Big Al's
How To Create A
Recruiting Explosion

by
Tom Schreiter

KAAS Publishing
P.O. Box 890084
Houston, TX 77289

D1113699

Printed in the United States of America.

ISBN 1-892366-01-0

Cover Design: Bruce McDonald & Alaine Roberts

About The Author

The eccentricity of the author was first noted in his early childhood. Through good nutrition, these strange traits were enhanced and nurtured to their present levels of obnoxious unbearableness. When asked if he had ever been serious in his life he replied, "What? Are you kidding?"

In addition to this fine work, *How To Create A Recruiting Explosion*, Tom Schreiter has also authored *Turbo MLM* and *Big Al Tells All*, which are musts for any serious MLMer. These equally awesome books are available for the unreasonably, ridiculously low, low price of $12.95 each, which includes shipping, handling, goodwill, this blatant commercial...oh yes, and the actual book.

Table of Contents

Rebuilding momentum

Your group is tired. No "get-up-and-go." The same three people attend your weekly meetings. Your group discussions are about company politics and the "good old days," not about future plans and goals. You are keeping most of your loyal distributors, but they aren't doing anything. Your group volume decreases slightly every month. Your organization has matured and growth is a thing of the past. Even your last training meeting had the same three distributors attending. If it weren't for depression, your group would have no emotion.

Multilevel groups are always on the move. Either they grow or they shrink. It's impossible to freeze your group's success. If your group is not growing - you have a problem.

Want to guarantee your group's decline? It's easy. Just stop working and watch. Your group will do the following:

1. Stop recruiting and start evaluating. "Hey, let's get a grip on things here. I think I should sit back and take a hard look at my business, you know, do a little planning."

2. Watch their volumes decline. Unfortunately, evaluating does not qualify as a business building tool. Recruiting and retailing activities build business.

3. Become negative because their volumes declined. Everyone gets on edge when volumes decline. Negative attitudes produce the next step.

4. Big reductions in volume. Our group responds to our leadership. When we take on a negative attitude, they will respond in a like manner. Having a consistent negative attitude throughout our group will produce consistent negative results; lower volume, less recruiting, etc.

5. Confirm negative attitudes. We *definitely* notice the depression and lethargy in our downline. We are observing facts.

6. Predict a dire future. With consistent, lower volumes, bad attitudes, and lack of motivation in our groups, we predict bad things to come.

7. Accelerated volume reduction. Our plans and predictions are working efficiently. The reduced volumes are feeding the negative attitudes, which produce even smaller volumes, which intensify the negative attitudes, etc.

8. Start a death march. Our three loyal distributors confirm at our next meeting that business is declining, soon to be dead. We are dealing with facts.

Chances are we would consider the above scenario a problem.

So, how do we build enthusiasm, initiative, and momentum? We know that excessive analysis and planning leads to group paralysis. So, we must focus specific energy to increase our group's growth pattern.

"This month — analysis. Next month — planning. Then, I'll start goal-setting. Managers don't have time for action."

Growth generates enthusiasm. People get excited when positive things happen. Everyone wants to associate with winners. So, to produce growth in our organization, all we have to do is *bring in new people*. That's the only way. It is next to impossible to rejuvenate "old distributors" once they have drifted into mediocrity. Modern science is without a cure. Training and rallies only give them a one or two day "hype", but nothing to sustain growth.

As leaders, we can control enthusiasm, initiative, and momentum for at least 7 days by using a simple little contest that **brings in new blood, creates excitement, and has long lasting results**.

But not just any contest will do. This is the key to creating the excitement. Too many leaders just run the contest and ignore the principles necessary to get the **desired results.** Let's quickly review why many contests are eligible for the *Hall of Shame.*

A. Only one person wins. If you have one distributor with exceptional talent, the rest of your distributors won't even try. They feel your talented distributor will win the contest anyway; so why bother trying? The results of your contest will be mediocre if you only have one distributor trying. The best contests have provisions that allow everyone to win. After all, you want to keep everyone trying and involved. The original purpose of having a contest was to increase productive activity, thereby increasing profitable results.

B. The qualifications are unattainable. If the standards necessary to win are perceived as impossible, again no one will try. Too many leaders set unrealistic standards, hoping to get more production. The opposite result occurs, no production, since no one is trying.

C. The activity required to win the contest has no long term or productive use. For example, a contest based on attending the most opportunity meetings. Attending opportunity meetings isn't productive – attending with guests is productive. A better contest would be based on bringing the most guests to opportunity meetings. Too many contests have the wrong activity to reach the desired production goals.

D. The contest periods are too long. Distributors, like ordinary people, are short-term planners. How many people do you know that plan ahead one year? Don't most people wait until the last minute to get a birthday card or gift? If your contests are longer than two weeks, distributors will wait thirteen days before starting. There have been successful contests for leaders that last up to one year, but we are dealing with beginning, unmotivated distributors. They want instant results and immediate rewards. A contest can be as short as a few hours, but never longer than a month.

E. The contest goals are the end, not the means. Too many leaders focus on the desired results. Instead, they should focus on how to get there.

Let's say that we want a larger product volume in our business. We could announce a contest that awards prizes for the largest product volumes. This is an inefficient way to approach it. Why? We haven't given our distributors the direction (the "Means") to get there. Our distributors will spend days sitting, planning, and trying to figure out the best way to get more product volume (the "End").

A better way is to base the contest on the ACTIVITY (the "Means") that would best achieve our desired goal. What if we thought it over and decided this:

The best way to get increased product movement is to get more distributors. If we have more distributors, they will personally use more product. Plus, after using the products, they will want to tell their friends about them. That means retail sales. Therefore, the best way to get more product volume (the "End") is to get more new distributors (the "Means") into our organization.

So let's run a contest to get more new distributors in our organization. The higher product volume will naturally follow.

We will do the planning and pre-thinking for our distributors. They won't have to waste valuable time determining their best course of action.

F. There is misunderstanding of inner motivations. Many leaders think distributors work hard to earn the prize at the end of the contest. The truth? The prize is a secondary motivator for contest participants. What do people want most? Recognition. People will work harder and longer for the recognition of winning, than for any prize yet developed. Distributors like being admired.

For example, consider the old "Steak & Beans" contest. At the beginning of the week, two distributors agree to the following:

Whoever sells the most product by Friday night gets to eat a steak dinner. The loser gets to eat beans. Plus, the loser must pay for both dinners and watch the victorious distributor enjoy his steak.

You'll be astonished how hard distributors will work just to win this contest. The best part is that the loser usually desires a rematch next week to restore his honor. That means more production. All this productive effort occurs - just for **recognition**.

The best part is that this contest costs practically nothing, yet consistently produces high results.

The moral? You can save a lot of money on prizes if you work recognition into the final contest prize.

G. The contest fails to teach a skill. Our contest should focus on business-building activities. Then, our distributors will be practicing and perfecting the skills needed for their success. When the contest is over, our distributors have finished an on-the-job training program. Now we are getting two birds with one stone - (not original).

The list of contest rules could go on and on, but at least these basics can ensure our contest's success.

Now for the greatest contest in multilevel marketing, (or at least a very good one). This contest uses many of the above rules and succeeds in getting distributor participation. This contest will produce enthusiasm, initiative, and momentum. What else could we possibly ask for in management? The contest works like this:

Let's say you have two unmotivated first level distributors. They haven't sponsored anyone in months. If you could just get a couple of new, excited distributors under them, you know they'd be excited. So now you need a contest that produces new distributors quickly.

The rules:

Each of your two first level, unmotivated distributors must sponsor a new distributor. Then, they must help their new distributor build six levels deep. This means your unmotivated distributors would have seven new distributors in their group, one on each level. The winning distributor is the first to get a 7th level distributor from his new downline.

All the emphasis is on depth – not width. The best way to win this contest is to sponsor just one person. Then, tell the new recruit about the contest and show how he will soon have six new distributors under him (the stairstep method). Next, ask the new distributor for a good referral and immediately get his referral into the business. Tell the newly sponsored referral about the contest and how he soon will have five new distributors under him. Then, ask him to give you a new lead or referral.

Just by going from one distributor to another, it will only take a few days to be seven levels deep. And it is easy. *No one had to get more than one person.*

Now, to make the contest fair, you offer to be the Big Al for both of your contestants. All they have to do is call when they need your help for presentations.

Why this contest works:

1. Your contestants are not alone. They feel motivated because they can count on your help. People work better in pairs.

2. All your contestant has to do is to get the first new prospect. *How hard can it be to sponsor someone when you tell him he is going to have six new distributors in his group in just a few days?* The rest of the leads will come from each new person sponsored.

3. You are promoting the "means" (the activity), not the "end" (the result). The result, more distributors and volume, will come naturally from the recruiting activity. One specific activity, sponsoring the first distributor, will get them started. The desired "end" result, getting your original distributors excited, occurs from the new and growing group.

4. Everyone is a winner. Even the distributor who loses will gain something (several new, excited distributors).

5. The benefits of the contest are long-lasting. You continue to receive profit month after month on the volume of your new distributors. Your old distributors become active again.

6. The contest doesn't grow old. You can run this contest again and again. Wouldn't it be fun to run this contest every month?

7. The contest is short and fun. Sometimes the contest is over in 24-48 hours. It motivates distributors to **immediate action.**

8. When the contest is over, the contestants have improved their recruiting skills. They gain added self-confidence with successful completion of a short-term goal.

There are many contests you can run to motivate your group. However, this contest contains the basic rules for contest success. Your contestants' initiative and immediate action will excite your entire group. In this contest, everyone is a winner.

The checklist close

"Well, let me think it over," comments your prospect at the end of the opportunity meeting. You don't want to high pressure your prospect, but what can you do to help make up his mind?

Can your prospect get any additional facts at home about your business to make a better decision? Will his spouse be able to evaluate the marketing plan and give an accurate assessment of the company's management? Do you really think your prospect will remember every detail of the opportunity meeting? Will he be able to explain the marketing plan's subtle features to his spouse?

Can your prospect get accurate multilevel advice from his lawyer or accountant? (If they really understood multilevel, they would be distributors already.) Why ask multilevel advice from someone trained in law or bookkeeping? We certainly don't ask accountants and lawyers for plumbing advice.

Wouldn't it benefit your prospect to make a decision now, while the facts are still fresh in his mind? And right now he has you available to answer any questions.

So, how do we get the prospect to make a decision now?

We use the **checklist close**.

The **checklist close** is a simple form that you make up to review the key points of the opportunity meeting. You simply review this form with your prospect before he leaves the meeting. At the end of the review, the prospect normally makes his decision to join.

Let's look at a sample form for Acme Corporation's Cleaning Products Division. We'll call your prospect, Mike.

Mike: "Well, I'll have to go home and think about this."

Distributor: "It's always good to review the facts. Acme gives us a form that I need to review with you tonight. This makes sure you receive all the pertinent facts about our business opportunity.

THE FORM

PRODUCT:

1. Do you see the need for the product?

2. Do you see how our product will save people money?

3. What do you think of the quality of our products?

4. Do you think our unique products are what people really want?

5. Were you impressed that our *Super Clean* was more effective than any product sold today?

6. How many people do you know would like to save money on their cleaning products?

7. Do you like to save money on your cleaning products?

8. Do you see how becoming a distributor can save you an additional 30% on the products you personally use?

9. Were you impressed with our "on the spot" 100% money back guarantee?

10. Have you ever seen a guarantee better than that?

11. Did you think the cleaning demonstration was impressive?

12. Do you see now why our products are selling so well?

TRAINING

1. What do you think of our guaranteed training program?

2. Do you see how our on-the-job training is better than just classroom training alone?

3. Did you like the part that in the beginning your sponsor builds your business while you observe?

4. Do you think it makes sense to observe and learn before you start on your own?

5. Our training workshop is a concentrated success builder. Do you think it makes sense to attend?

6. Do you like the constant availability of our Regional Manager for specialized training?

7. If you decided to take advantage of this business opportunity, would you use the training available?

MARKETING

1. As a distributor, do you see that you receive a permanent 30% discount on personal purchases?

2. By buying wholesale, and then selling at retail, do you see that you earn a 30% profit on all of your sales?

3. Do you like the idea that you can sponsor others and earn additional bonuses on their purchases?

4. If you become involved with our business, would you like to earn the top position of Manager?

5. What did you think of the company car program? Would you and your wife want an additional new car?

6. As a manager, you order direct from the home office. Do you see the income advantages of ordering in bulk at additional discounts?

7. Did you like the fact that our business only takes 10-12 hours a week?

8. Many of our distributors started part-time. When their earnings exceeded their full-time job, they quit their jobs to devote all their time to their business. Would you like this opportunity to produce a full-time income?

9. Do you see that you have everything to gain and nothing to lose in our *guaranteed fast start program*?

After reviewing the company's checklist, the conversation goes like this:

Distributor: Are there any other questions? Is it all clear to you?

Mike: Seems pretty clear.

Distributor: Fine, let's get started on the "guaranteed fast start program." Then you can take some samples and study material home tonight. I know you will find this business exciting.

Mike: Sounds good. Hey, I have everything to gain.

The **checklist close** is effective because it eliminates one of the major reasons why new prospects don't join — confusion. After a typical opportunity meeting, the new prospect is dazzled by all the facts. He reacts by stalling for time to sort the information. However, the prospect benefits if he can make a decision with all the facts. That means you should be at his side to answer any questions. Why not give your prospects the best possible chance for an intelligent personal decision? Use the **checklist close.**

The pressure is on

Dear Big Al,

I am a new distributor just getting started in multilevel marketing. I just moved to a new town and don't know anyone. I want to build a strong multilevel business. Since I have no experience in multilevel marketing, I don't know where to start or what to do.

I heard you are the ultimate mentor, the number one pro in the industry. That's why I am writing you. I won't ask for much, and I won't take much of your time. You don't have time to take on an additional protege, so I will ask for only one favor.

Would you please come to my town for JUST ONE DAY, and get me off to a quick start? Just teach me one technique and I will build my business from that starting point. I'm a self starter, so you'll never have to hear from me again.

That's it. Just give me one day and I'll be forever in your debt.

Sincerely,

Jerry Aggressive (Brand New Distributor)

What a letter! What would you do if you got this letter? This motivated self starter could really make your business grow. We enjoy getting letters from motivated people. All he wants is just **one little miracle!**

It is hard for a new distributor to build a group. It takes trial and error, workshops and training seminars, retailing, prospecting, leadership, and more. Several months may pass with little or no progress. There will be ups and downs. Product shipments may be late. Meetings may be hard to organize. It will take time to build a large and dedicated group to have exciting meetings.

We have to build deep to help our new distributor taste some success. And since our brand new, inexperienced distributor knows nothing about our business, our task can be overwhelming.

All our new distributor wants is to have a successful, excited, large organization of new distributors NOW. And he is generous; he is going to give us ONE WHOLE DAY to work our miracle. He wants to bypass months of work to become an instant leader of an excited distributor organization.

Well, this is the challenge of leadership. Since new distributors hold us in high esteem, we are **expected** to work miracles.

So, what do we do for one day that will accomplish all of our new distributor's objectives? Do we run an ad? Tell him to make a few hundred new friends before we arrive? Do we put on a suit of armor and go door to door begging people to become distributors? Or, how about giving him a catchy slogan on a lapel button? We can tell him to walk around shopping malls and hope prospects will mob him with distributor applications. Maybe we could mail out flyers to people in the phone book and hope they send us orders. With only one day to perform a miracle, our options are limited.

So here is the test. *What would you do?* (Skipping town or faking illness is not an acceptable option. Upline leaders are suppose to be heroes.)

The stair step solution

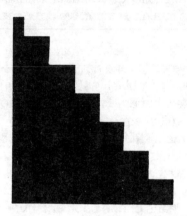

Dear Jerry,

It is always a pleasure to hear from a motivated self-starter. I appreciated your attitude to go out on your own and be responsible for your financial future.

Yes, my schedule is tight and my open time is very limited. However, I'm looking forward to this opportunity to help you get off to a great start. I appreciate your desire to learn streamlined and efficient ways to build your business. Too many new distributors use trial and error to reinvent the wheel.

Here is my one requirement for coming to help you for the day:

Make an appointment with two or three people to spend five minutes with me. Just tell them that I wish to interview them about the business climate in their area. You may also tell them the name of our company or answer any other questions they may have. I just wish to ask them a few questions.

If you do your part, I'll guarantee you will have up to 20 people in your organization in just a few days. We won't have enough time to get all 20 on the day I am with you. However, I'll build the foundation and give you the technique to finish the job.

I am looking forward to our day together next week.

Sincerely,

Big Al

The day of reckoning arrived the following week. Big Al arrived early to meet Jerry and his first prospect at the local restaurant. His prospect, John, was a local businessman and a member of the Jaycees. He had welcomed Jerry to the community just a few days after Jerry received Big Al's acceptance letter.

Big Al asked John if he was familiar with multilevel marketing. John was aware of this type of business and once attended an exciting opportunity meeting. The opportunity meeting lasted over two hours and John had to leave before it was over. He decided not to join because if meetings took that long, there wouldn't be enough time to work the business.

Big Al explained a little about the company and how the meetings were only 40 minutes. John said he had enough time for some additional details, so Big Al gave a quick 20 minute presentation.

At the end of the presentation John said, "Very interesting. I'll go home and think it over for a few days."

Then Big Al dropped the *stair step close*.

"John, you know that Jerry is just opening up the opportunity in this area. We will put 20 new distributors into the organization over the next few days. We would like them all to be in your downline. This would give you a tremendous start and you could provide some good, stable leadership for them. Would you please give me the correct spelling of your last name and your social security number so the next person we talk to will get you as his sponsor?"

Big Al wrote down the name and social security number in the sponsor section of a blank application. Next, he handed John a blank application to fill out. Jerry just stared in amazement. Finally, Big Al filled in the proper information for a product purchase so John would have some experience with the product line.

Secretly, Jerry wondered, "Why did John change his mind so quickly? Was it the promise of 20 people in his downline? How are we going to get 20 people to keep this commitment? We don't know anyone in this town."

When John finished the paperwork Big Al said, "John, as you can see this is a great opportunity. I know you probably have a close friend or business associate that you would like to help. As long as we are going to be building this organization of new distributors under you, maybe we should enroll your friend next. Then he will also benefit from this group of distributors."

John replied, "That's a great idea. My best friend Mike has always wanted to be in a part-time business and earn extra money. Your efforts in getting new distributors would get him off to a guaranteed fast start and really build his confidence! Let's get him on the phone now and sign him up before you get the rest of the distributors."

John called Mike on the restaurant's pay phone. Mike asked that Big Al and Jerry hurry over to his house before he left for work. If John said it was a good deal, and there was a guaranteed quick start, he wanted to sign up now.

Big Al thanked John for his time. "Remember, the first meeting for this area is one week from today."

Big Al and Jerry jumped in Big Al's car and quickly drove over to Mike's house.

On the way over, Jerry commented, "That's incredible! The first person we talked to sponsored, gave us a product order, and referred us to a presold distributor prospect. I think the promise of 20 distributors in his downline had a lot to do with it. What really puzzles and bothers me is that you and I together know less than 3 people in this town. How are we going to keep our commitment?"

Big Al replied, "Observe closely, and see what your conclusions are at the end of the day. Let's visit Mike and see what we learn from him."

Mike was the easiest presentation Jerry could imagine. He had his pen out ready to sign the application when he answered the doorbell. Obviously, his respect for John, and John's enthusiasm had completely presold Mike before they arrived.

At the end of the brief presentation Big Al said, "Mike, as John told you, we are concentrating our effort in bringing in new distributors over the next few days. In fact, we are going to be putting 19 new distributors into your organization to give you a fast start. I am sure you have a friend or close business associate who would like to take advantage of this fast start. We could put distributors into his organization while still helping you. Your friend would thank you for this opportunity. Who do you know that deserves and would appreciate this fast start in his own part-time business?"

Mike quickly answered, "I've been thinking the very same thing since my conversation with John earlier this morning. My brother Jim could be good in this business. I always wanted to help him get ahead, and this would be the perfect opportunity. Let me call him now and see if you can go right over. I certainly want you to sign him up before you get the other new distributors. I really want him up on top. He could be the next superstar for this company."

Mike's brother Jim said Big Al and Jerry could meet him at work in 15 minutes. He could take a little break to visit with them and see what they had to offer.

The appointment with Jim was a bit more challenging. Jim got excited about the help in building his downline and that John and Mike had already signed up. Being in on the ground floor in his area was a pretty good deal too.

Big Al closed by saying, "Jim, when it came down to one person that Mike wanted to help, he chose you. Mike knew that you would appreciate our efforts in giving you a fast start in building your downline. We plan to put 18 new distributors into your downline over the next few days. Who do you want at the top of your organization?"

Jim replied, "Big Al, there are two people that I feel would take advantage and really work this program, especially with the extra help you offer. First, my boss here at work. He is always looking to improve his finances. The other prospect is my next door neighbor Allen. Would it be possible for my boss to sponsor Allen, and you continue to build under Allen? That way your efforts would benefit not only me, but also my boss and Allen."

"No problem," said Big Al. He and Jerry went upstairs and introduced Jim's boss to the program. At the end of the presentation, Jim's boss wanted to think it over. Big Al said, "We will need your name and social security number as the sponsor for Allen. Allen is Jim's next door neighbor. Jim wanted you to be his sponsor so all of Allen's efforts would benefit you." Jim's boss filled out the application.

Before leaving to see Allen, Big Al said to Jim's boss, "Since we are going to put 17 new distributors into your organization over the next few days, who would you like to benefit from this effort? If you have a friend or close business associate that you would like at the top of these new distributors, let's talk to him right away so he benefits, too."

Jim's boss answered, "I appreciate that Jim wants me to sponsor his next door neighbor, Allen. To show my appreciation, I am going to sponsor my three best friends under Allen. That way your recruiting efforts can continue under my three friends and benefit all of us. Let me get them on the phone and make the appointments."

And so the day went. Jerry observed the master of multilevel marketing in action. By that evening, Big Al and Jerry had sponsored 14 new distributors. With only a few more distributors needed to reach their goal of 20, Jerry was confident that next week's first meeting was going to be great.

"I see how you keep your commitments to help people off to a fast start," said Jerry. "You can go home early. I can finish this job. There are enough leads to finish up the remaining six distributors needed to fulfill our commitments. This simple technique will build me an organization beyond my wildest dreams. I only have one first level distributor now, but there will be a total of 20 distributors in my group for next week's meeting. And the best part is everyone will be excited because they have distributors in their downline. I'm not worried about having only one first level. Starting next week I am going to sponsor my second first level distributor. And guess what? I'll work with my second first level until he has 20 in his downline, too."

"Today was a miracle for me, Big Al. I saw 15 presentations, and 14 joined. I now have a growing, excited organization. And all this in just ONE DAY! Now I see how an upline leader should work. I am going to follow your footsteps and show my organization how to do the same."

Big Al left Jerry to finish up this recruiting campaign. Sometimes working miracles was not as easy as today.

Work smart, not hard

Professional recruiters spend time in front of **qualified** prospects. Amateurs spend time in front of anyone and everyone. To give you an idea of the inefficiency of making presentations to unqualified prospects, let's look at the following example.

Joe Distributor's appointments take about two hours each. The actual presentation is only 30 or 40 minutes, but travel time and waiting time add an extra 1½ hours. This means that Joe can only make two appointments per evening after he leaves his job. If Joe Distributor makes 10 appointments with unqualified prospects, he wastes an entire week. This is how discouragement can begin to grow.

What professional recruiters need is a system to rate or measure prospects. We don't want to waste hours with impossible, unqualified prospects. That's working hard, not smart.

What if we worked with just one good, qualified prospect each week? Our results would be far greater than making hopeless presentations to 10 unqualified, time-wasting prospects. Keeping busy making presentations doesn't count; making presentations to qualified prospects pays the bills.

Just think of the mileage we get from one good, qualified prospect. Our superstar can build 30 or 40 distributors quickly. Our hopeless prospects will spend the same time whining why the opportunity isn't working for them.

This is why professional recruiters separate their prospects into 3 categories.

Category A: Qualified prospects with potential. These prospects can make our business boom. Our job is to locate them. They are potential leaders and self starters.

Category B: Prospects that have possibilities. There is a 50/50 chance that they could be worthwhile, or a complete waste of time.

Category C: Worthless, time-wasting, unqualified prospects. Losers spend their time trying to re-program these time wasters.

The business of **sorting** prospects into three categories is not difficult. It can make the difference between success and failure. The following test illustrates how easy **sorting** can be. Quickly review the following brief seven situations. Classify the prospect as **A, B,** or **C.** Then, write down the reasons for your assessment. This exercise will launch your career as a professional recruiter.

Situation 1

You are walking down a street and see a well-dressed man walking towards you. He is happy, positive and looks like good fortune has favored him. He waves and greets the people passing. He has the look of leadership about him. As you approach him, what category of prospect would he fall into? A, B, or C?

Situation 2

As you walk further down the street, you trip over a man lying in the gutter. The smell of alcohol is everywhere and he is holding a cracked bottle of cheap wine. His clothes are a mess and he is obviously not "all there" as he mumbles in confusion. What category: A, B, or C?

Situation 3

You stop at the phone company to ask about your bill. They refer you to the stereotype accountant. With wire glasses, a green visor, and garters on his sleeves, he looks like he belongs inside a calculator, not in the real world. He is shy, but obviously enjoys his work of adding and subtracting numbers. What category: A, B or C?

Situation 4

A young hippie offers to sell you drugs. She obviously is her own best customer, but insists you try her quality

products. She is aggressive with great sales skills. What category: A, B or C?

Situation 5

Continuing down the street you see a lady, visibly upset. She kicks a small kitten across the street and punches a passing girl scout. The lady curses the world and anyone within listening range. This is a negative, angry person. What category: A, B or C?

Situation 6

A young boy, age 16, passes by. He is talking with his friends about tonight's high school rally. His goal is to get a date for the rally. What category: A, B or C?

Situation 7

You meet a pleasant lady at the checkout counter of the neighborhood drug store. She is courteous, helpful and positive. What category: A, B or C?

"What professional recruiters need is a system to rate or classify prospects."

The answers

Situation 1

The happy, well-dressed man coming towards you has a reason for being happy. He just robbed the 1st National Bank. With his superb leadership abilities, he assembled a crack group of bank-robbing criminals. He is acting friendly and calm so the police will not suspect him as a fleeing criminal. Any legitimate method of earning money is repulsive to him. In short, he is a louse.

Situation 2

The man lying in the gutter has just moved to your city. He is the National Sales Manager for a large corporation. He was just mugged, hit over the head with a cheap wine bottle! He is not fully conscious or coherent, but if he were, he would ask to join your multilevel company. He feels that is a better way to meet new people in a strange city.

Situation 3

Mr. Accountant secretly plots to leave his job and start his own accounting and tax business. Every evening he looks for part-time work to supplement his business start-up fund. He hopes to find a part-time business that will provide extra income to support the early years of his business. He will continue to search for a part-time opportunity until some imaginative person sees his need.

Situation 4

You are right. This young hippie has no place in your organization. However, if you would ask for referrals, you would meet her mother. She needs part-time income for her daughter's bail and rehabilitation. A super prospect.

Situation 5

This disturbed lady was the administrative assistant of a large corporation. She ran the company while her boss took all the credit. He fired her twenty minutes ago without severance pay. She knows she'll never work for anybody again. As soon as she has a drink to calm her nerves, she will be looking for her own business. No more bosses! No more time clocks! No more measly salary for her efforts!

Situation 6

This young man is a member of the Junior Achievement Club. He has a sales personality and needs some money to buy his first car. His uncle once headed several thousand distributors for a multilevel company and would like to help his nephew get started in a multilevel business.

Situation 7

The girl at the checkout counter is working nights to earn extra money. Since she earns less than $5 an hour, she is open to any recruiting presentation. She wants more money and more time with her family.

Unfair! Unfair! Unfair!

Wait a minute! Is this some kind of a trick? There wasn't enough information to know that the seven situations would end up like that. What's the deal?

The previous test can be summed up in the very original phrase:

YOU CAN'T JUDGE A BOOK BY ITS COVER.

If the moral to this exercise is "don't prejudge", what can we do as professional recruiters to solve this problem?

As professionals, we realize we must spend our time only with A and B prospects. The challenge is: "How do we know who is an A or B prospect without wasting a lot of time?"

The answer: **PROFESSIONAL ICEBREAKERS.**

Let's first define an icebreaker. An icebreaker is a conversation starter, something that guides the conversation to a desired topic. The secret is to have the icebreaker give you enough information to determine if your prospect is an A, B, or C.

To give you a better idea, let's consider a young single man wishing to meet a young lady at a social event. The young man must first start a conversation and guide the conversation to a desired end. Part of his icebreaker aims to find out if the young lady is single or married. If married, this qualifies the young lady as a C prospect. If the young lady responds to his initial conversation with, "Get lost, dog breath!", this may also qualify the young lady as a C prospect. What kind of icebreakers would this young man use?

"What's a nice lady like you doing in a place like this?" Corny, semi-effective. The young lady must respond. She may even smile at this old cliche.

Or, "Haven't I seen you someplace before?" While neither of these icebreakers are original, they both get the conversation going. They also get the conversation guided in the right direction.

So, what kind of icebreaker can we use in multilevel marketing? Let's look at some ineffective ones first.

The most hated award? "Nice day out today." Absolutely awful. It is trite, leads nowhere, and leaves the prospect wondering what you are up to. The big problem is what do you say next? How about, "Nice day out today, do you want to be a multilevel distributor?" Your prospects won't die of overexcitement.

Or, "Say, what are you doing Tuesday night?" How would you feel if someone asked you that question? Apprehensive? Would you feel that you are being set up for an unpleasant experience on Tuesday night?

One solution to the professional icebreaker dilemma is the *Two Magic Questions*. (See *Big Al Tells All* for a complete explanation of this powerful icebreaker.) In the ten seconds it takes to use this icebreaker, we break the ice and qualify our prospect as either an A, B, or C prospect! This is the power of the *Two Magic Questions* icebreaker and why professional recruiters use it regularly. Why guess or waste time on C prospects when the 10 second *Two Magic Questions* icebreaker will solve our sorting problem?

The bottom line is: Don't prejudge your prospects. Use the *Two Magic Questions* approach to become a professional, efficient recruiter.

Locate the fishing hole

A wide, shallow stream flows through the meadow. The stream is only six inches deep. However, further downstream it settles into a lovely, deep, clear pool.

Now, it's your day to go fishing. Where would you cast your line? In the shallow, fast moving stream? Or, would you cast your line in the deep pool that offers the fish both food and safety? (Hint: pick the second choice.)

There are two rules for becoming a great fisherman:

1. Cast your line where the fish are.

2. Tell great stories about the one that got away.

Let's talk about rule one and how it applies to multilevel recruiting. Have you ever seen amateur recruiters? Their continued wasted effort is enough to make their sponsors cry. The reason for their failures and discouragements? *They are fishing where there ain't no fish!*

Some samples of inefficient recruiting activities could be:

1. Mailing a 2 lb. package of literature, brochures, catalogs etc. to everyone in the local phone book. Certainly there are prospects in every town, but only a small percentage are quality prospects. Only a few people wait by their mailboxes for the perfect multilevel offer.

A quality mailing list gets the message in front of more qualified prospects. However, mailing list, postage and printing costs will discourage even the hardiest new recruit. Poor net returns will sink the spirits of any downliner. So, even a quality mailing is usually wasted. Most of the packages will go to "fishless" waters.

2. Standing on a corner passing out product samples to disinterested pedestrians. The distributor hopes the people will use and fall in love with his product. He is disappointed when the phone doesn't ring constantly with excited, delirious prospects begging to join his multilevel company.

3. Driving 450 miles to paste up flyers in every grocery store bulletin board in the county. The distributor is sure that every housewife exiting the store with 3 pre-schoolers and 5 bags of groceries wants to join his multilevel opportunity. The distributor spends the next week babysitting the phone, wondering why no one is calling.

4. Going to the unemployment office and announcing, "Anyone who wants to lose his weekly benefits check, please contact me about a business opportunity." The response is underwhelming. The distributor then questions the validity of his opportunity, because no one took him up his offer.

5. Asking his relatives to give up bowling to come to his opportunity meeting. Then his upline sponsor, *Good ol' Distributor* tells the audience his latest get-rich plan. Since *Good ole Distributor* has never been rich, or even in business, the audience leaves to go bowling.

So where *are* the fish?

Professional recruiters prospect where the fish are so thick you can walk across the pond. Why waste time fishing where the fish are scarce?

Elaborate, expensive recruiting campaigns are not the answer. The secret is simple: creative recruiting campaigns where all the prospects are great prospects!

Unfortunately, creative thought is a lost art. They say, "People are lost in thought because it is unfamiliar territory." Yet creative thought can give phenomenal recruiting results. Just stop and think "Where are the *most* and *best* prospects?"

To illustrate the power of creative thought, here is what a young lady, Dorothy, did a few years ago.

Dorothy was a beautician, pigeon-holed into a limited earning potential. Even with limited free time, she knew multilevel was for her. All she needed was to start an effecive recruiting program that took little personal time.

Her customers didn't want a long-term business with long-term rewards. They focused on today's TV Guide. Why work and wait to get paid? Maybe there's a deal that would pay them before they worked. Sure, it's an outside chance, but definitely worth waiting for. Her beauty customers were C prospects.

With only two nights a week free, where could Dorothy go to build a group of go-getters fast?

Dorothy developed a brilliant solution. The local Chamber of Commerce sponsored a Free School of Business in the evenings at a local college. The free school performed a valuable service of educating adults about the value of free enterprise. Among the many business and accounting courses offered, there was a course on sales and marketing. Dorothy and three of her new distributors enrolled in the Tuesday night course.

Dorothy and her distributors learned many sales and marketing techniques. However, they enrolled because this class was a prime prospecting nest of quality winners. Every Tuesday evening they practiced their presentation skills and met other class members. Dorothy felt this was the best place to prospect because:

1. All the participants were salesmen or future salesmen. Her fellow classmates would be outgoing, uninhibited, and have no prejudice against direct sales.

2. Her fellow classmates had a strong *desire* to improve themselves and their earning power. They made personal sacrifices to give up an evening to learn new skills.

3. Her fellow classmates wanted a better life. They were not satisfied with the rewards from their present occupations. They were looking for answers and solutions to reach their income goals.

This creative way of locating quality prospects had two additional benefits for Dorothy and her distributors:

1. The price was right. The course was free!

2. Dorothy and her distributors also learned some terrific selling skills that would help them throughout their careers.

Recruiting class members was easy. They just mentioned a few benefits that appealed to their classmates' needs. For example:

1. Their business opportunity could create a steady income stream. While the income would initially be small, every month it would build. In time, the part-time business could provide an excellent base income. This income could shield salesmen from the ups and downs of a commission-based job.

The salesmen and their spouses felt this benefit alone warranted instant action. They wanted to start building their multilevel business now.

2. A multilevel business, when built with a solid foundation, can provide an excellent income every month. Even if you discontinued working the program, your residual income would continue. It's almost like having a disability insurance income whether you are sick or not.

A salesman's income stops when he can't make sales calls. Plus, it feels great to wake up at the beginning of a month with a guaranteed income. Any extra effort for the month will improve this guaranteed income.

3. Everyone likes extra income monthly. Dorothy pointed out that a modest $500 extra per month from a part-time multilevel business could be exciting. A person would have to have $60,000 in a bank earning 10% interest to get an extra $500 a month. Dorothy asked her classmates, "How hard would it be for you to accumulate an extra $60,000 in your bank account?" They said it would be easier to build a part-time business than to save $60,000.

4. Building a part-time multilevel business is risk-free. Her classmates could continue their full-time, commissioned sales jobs until their part-time business earnings exceeded their full-time earnings! What a great way to achieve financial independence! No heavy investment or risk!

The payoff? Dorothy and her distributors sponsored 26 of the 43 class members, as well as the instructor! Dorothy not only reached the highest level in her company in just 30 days, but exceeded the requirements by over 300%.

When asked if building a multilevel business was hard, Dorothy replied, "It's like shooting fish in a barrel."

The magic beans

Once upon a time, there was an idiot. The idiot was conned out of his possessions for some magic beans. Thus we have the story of *Jack and the Beanstalk*.

This story is not about him.

Distributor Joe explained to Big Al that his group was becoming complacent.

"They just haven't sponsored any new blood. Nothing seems to work. I've tried bribes, contests, friendly persuasion, and they just won't set goals or recruit. I am baffled. Any suggestions, Big Al?"

Big Al replied, "You noticed that the business is no longer fun for your distributors, eh? No fun means no production, Joe. This looks like a great time for your mediocre distributors to reset some goals."

"Well, I've tried to make them reset some goals, but they just don't respond. I know that short-term goals are what they need, but how do I get them to set goals?"

"Joe, just set a fun activity and they will accomplish short term goals without even knowing it. Why not try the *Magic Bean* campaign? It is fun, and gets your distributors to **approach** new prospects. Once you get them approaching new prospects, the rest will fall into place."

"I'm ready, Big Al," said Joe, pulling out his note pad. "Just how does this miracle work?"

"First, buy a one pound bag of dry kidney beans. Then call a meeting of all your complacent distributors and say it is not a training or opportunity meeting. Tell them it is a special *Magic Bean* meeting. That will help improve attendance. Curiosity does bring people out."

"Now that I have a big group, I better do something good," commented Distributor Joe.

Big Al continued, "Start the meeting by telling them about the wonderful *Magic Beans* you have just received from your sponsor, Big Al. Explain that these beans are not just ordinary beans, but special beans that will make their distributorships grow. Because they are special, you are limiting each person to only three beans.

Next, explain how to use them. The beans work magic every time they are used correctly. First thing in the morning, put the 3 magic beans in your left pocket. Whenever you **approach** a new prospect and attempt to set an appointment, take one bean out of your left pocket and place it into your right pocket. It doesn't matter if you were successful in setting an appointment. The attempt qualifies you to move the bean from pocket to pocket.

The secret of the beans' magic is *you must move all 3 beans before the day ends.* This forces your distributors to make a minimum of three contacts daily. It's a fun, short-term goal. Their activity, approaching prospects, will result in some appointments. Presently, they have no appointments because they don't make contacts. Once they begin to make recruiting appointments, their confidence and enthusiasm will return."

Joe made a memo in his notebook: "Get two pounds of beans. A lot of work ahead."

Too good to be true

A man dies and goes up to the pearly gates. Saint Peter meets him at the gates and says:

"Come on into my office and sit down, we have a new program here. Our new program is that you have a choice."

The man replies, "That sounds great. Tell me about it."

Saint Peter continues, "Well, in our new program you can go up into heaven - but if you prefer, you can go down into the other place."

The man paused for a second and said, "Well, I am the type of guy who likes to check things out. Would it be okay if I take a look at both places? I certainly wouldn't want to make a decision without all the facts."

Saint Peter agreed, took the man up to heaven, and showed him around for a little while.

"Hey, it's pretty nice up here," commented the man. "It is quiet, serene, and peaceful. But you know, I'm quite an active guy, so would you mind if I took a look at the other place?"

"No problem," says Saint Peter. The two men went down to the "other place" and opened the door. The lights flashed, the music blared, people were drinking and dancing and having all kinds of fun.

"I just can't believe it. I never thought it would be like this! You know, I was kind of an old party guy back on earth. I really like this."

Saint Peter smiled and said, "Okay, let's go back into my office. It's time to make your decision."

The man went with Saint Peter to his office, sat down and said, "Well, heaven was really great. Nice and quiet, peaceful and serene. But you know, back on earth I really was a party animal. I never expected the 'other place' to be like that. Honestly, I am going to have to choose down below, the 'other place'."

Saint Peter replied, "We accept your decision. Come on down."

They went down below, opened the door, but this time flames roared out. Saint Peter pushed the man inside and slammed the door shut. A big guy grabbed the man and yelled, "Here's a shovel. Start shoveling coal."

After twenty minutes of shoveling coal into the furnace, the man stopped and looked at himself. He was dirty, hot, and sweaty. He looked to the big guy who gave him the shovel and said, " I don't understand this at all. A while ago I came down here and there was music, drinking and dancing. It was so wonderful. *WHAT HAPPENED?*"

The big guy turned to the man and said, "Ah, yes... well, that was our opportunity meeting!"

Today's prospects are sophisticated. They're smarter than many hucksters and promoters anticipate. If we over-sell our opportunity, we lose credibility with our potential distributors. Our prospects come to an opportunity meeting to hear a fair evaluation of a business opportunity. They don't want to hear a one-sided pep rally that borders on a carnival atmosphere.

Place yourself in a prospect's shoes. How would you feel if the audience applauded the speaker's every phrase? You would feel that you were sitting in a 'set up'. You wouldn't join because you felt you needed to hear the other side of the story.

Or what would happen if you did join? In a few days, reality would hit you squarely in the forehead. When you experienced the hard work it takes to achieve those fantastic incomes promised, you would feel deceived and resent-ful. Not a good attitude for success.

Can you avoid overselling and still get results? *YES, YES, YES!* You may experience even better results if you prac-tice a little underselling in your presentation.

Underselling builds credibility. Credibility builds trust. Isn't that what sponsoring is all about?

Don't say, "Every distributor sponsored becomes instant-ly rich and famous." Instead, let's look at how underselling can give us credibility and get a better commitment from our prospect.

For example, let's say we closed with this statement:

"Mr. Prospect, this is a wonderful opportunity, but only if you make an effort. I have several distributors in my group that make a 10% effort. They become discouraged and don't make the incomes possible in our business. Because they put forth only 10% effort, I can only commit 10% effort to help them. On the other hand, I have some distributors in my group who put forth 100% effort. They realize growing incomes and success. Because they put 100% of themselves into the business, I put 100% of myself into helping them succeed. Together, we do a pretty good job. In this business you get out of it what you put into it."

Now the decision is up to your prospect. He knows this business is not a free ride. He respects you for telling the truth — sharing the good and the bad. If he joins looking for a free ride and fails, he can't blame you. You told him up front it was his effort that would make the difference. And besides, you don't really want somebody looking for a free ride. Nobody benefits from freeloaders.

If your prospect joins and makes the 100% commitment, doesn't this make both the sponsor and the prospect winners?

Underselling will improve your sponsoring averages. People will join if they receive fair information, the good and the bad.

Why people don't believe you

Distributor Joe arrived at Big Al's home.

"I just can't understand it," Distributor Joe moaned, "it is unbelievable that my last appointment could turn me down. This business opportunity offers them everything they want in life and yet they turned it down. It is almost as if they were *satisfied* with their present misery!"

"I am afraid you answered your own riddle," Big Al replied. "Let's take a look why people act this way."

Big Al then began the story of *Tom and Ann Complacent*.

"Many years ago, I presented the opportunity of a lifetime to Tom and Ann Complacent. I found the possibilities of financial freedom through multilevel marketing so exciting that I challenged the Complacents. I told them to write down on a piece of paper the **things** most people wanted in life.They wrote the following:

Rolls Royce	**Mansion**	**Jet**
Yacht	**Stocks & Bonds**	**Real Estate**
$1,000,000	**Island**	**World Travel**
Diamonds	**Fur Coat**	**Ranch**

After writing down the things most people wanted in life, a strange thing happened."

Mr. Complacent said, "You know, we really wouldn't want to have a Rolls Royce. What would our friends think? They probably would feel we were being snobbish and trying to show off. Besides, we are true Americans. We would never buy an imported car. Our 1969 Plymouth suits us just fine."

Mrs. Complacent added, "And a mansion? No way. Just think of the real estate taxes and all the cleaning that comes with a house that size. That would mean moving from our neighborhood and friends. We certainly wouldn't want that. We enjoy renting our home. We really don't want the burden of owning."

"And jets are dangerous! You know the old saying, 'What goes up, must come down'. Well, I certainly want no part of flying."

Tom Complacent continued, "Yachts are nothing more than expensive toys. Where would we put it if we had one? We live hundreds of miles from the coast. The living quarters are cramped. You can get seasick. And, there is always the danger of hurricanes."

"I used to own some stocks. It was terrible. The price went down and I lost money. Plus, there is the day-to-day pressure of following the prices. It takes too much time and energy to keep track of investments."

"We used to have friends who owned an apartment building," added Mrs. Complacent. *"They went through hell. Tenants called them in the middle of the night with dripping faucets, the janitor quit, and all kind of difficulties. If we were rich, we certainly wouldn't want to own any real estate."*

"Do you realize the problems that rich people have? What if a person did get one million dollars? Just think of all the taxes he would have to pay. Also, the time spent with accountants, tax experts and the many relatives asking for loans, etc. Money certainly can't buy happiness, so we don't want any money getting in our way.

"An island? Are you kidding? Out in the middle of nowhere at the mercy of hurricanes? And no local TV stations? Only some yuppie lunatic could possibly want that."

"I don't know about world traveling," chimed in Mr. Complacent. *"You have to visit all those boring monuments, churches and go into squalid neighborhoods to visit the local populace. Besides, you know what they do to rich Americans traveling abroad, don't you? They kidnap them!"*

Mrs. Complacent went on, *"And if I had diamonds, I would be afraid to wear them in public. You know they are a target for thieves. If you have to keep them in a safety deposit box, what's the use of having them in the first place? Just think of how much the insurance premium would be on diamonds anyway."*

"I wouldn't be caught dead wearing a fur coat. Imagine what all those conservationists would say about killing wildlife for coats. My five-year old cloth coat from Sears still fits fine."

"Now, the most ridiculous thing of all is a ranch. On ranches you have horses and you have to take care of them. If we had a lot of money, we wouldn't want to spend the rest of our days shoveling horse manure!"

Distributor Joe smiled after hearing the story of the Complacents. They sounded like his last appointment. "It's amazing how people can kill their dreams and aspirations," commented Distributor Joe. "Just why and how do they do this? Why are some people just impossible to motivate?"

Big Al drew a large circle around all the things the Complacents wanted. "Let's call this their *dream circle*," said Big Al. "Everyone has a *dream circle* when they are young. Over here, let's draw the Complacent's *income circle*. This smaller circle represents the income they have to obtain

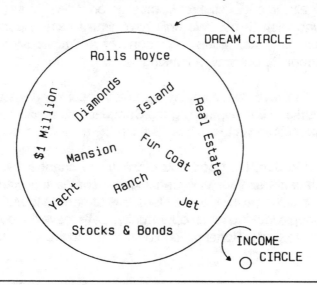

their dreams. Unfortunately, the dreams are too big to fit into the income circle, so the Complacents have to make an adjustment. They either have to *increase* their income to make their *income circle* larger, or they have to *decrease* the size of their *dream circle*. That is, they must eliminate some of their dreams."

Big Al summarized, "Tom and Ann Complacent probably had all these dreams when they got married. However, they fell in a rut of believing that financial freedom is only for the elite. They began to believe that being passed over for a promotion, not having the Midas touch or not winning the lottery, was going to be the way life goes. And all their friends and fellow employees were happy to confirm this. They would say how bad things were and they should just be happy with what they had. After years of brainwashing, all the Complacents' dreams went down the drain."

"The sad part is that it is almost impossible to help someone who has given up. It could take years of positive reinforcement to get the Complacents to believe in themselves again. In our business, we must go on to find those people who wish to try. We only have time to assist people in reaching their goals. We don't have time to reprogram people to our way of thinking."

"However, once you're financially secure and wish to do works of charity, helping the Complacents overcome their mental blocks to success is a worthy gift to humanity."

"So Joe, it's good you didn't try to change the Complacents to your way of thinking. That is the mark of a recruiting professional. Our job is to sort, to locate those people looking for an opportunity. Let's leave the convincing to professional psychologists and social workers."

Distributor Joe eats the office

"This is fantastic! All I have to do is sign here and the office is mine, right?"

Distributor Joe quickly signed the lease papers to his new downtown executive office. With his new centralized office, Joe knew his business would grow by leaps and bounds. The new office would give the professional image Joe needed. He could attract businessmen and professionals to build new, strong downlines. No more home meetings or *two-on-ones* for Joe; now he was going *big league.*

The new office was a financial sacrifice for Joe. There were deposits on the three-year lease and for utilities. Also, there were business phone installation charges, and a hefty monthly payment for the classic furniture. Even with a few other miscellaneous expenses, Joe felt the investment in his business was the right thing to do. And besides, who could resist the prestige of being in the tallest and newest building in town?

"I can hold regular leadership meetings here. Plus, my distributors will always know where to find me. Aggressive management decisions like these make real leaders," thought Distributor Joe.

One week later, Joe settled in and began his schedule. Since he couldn't afford a secretary to answer the phone, Joe had to be at the office from 9 AM to 5 PM. An answering machine wouldn't convey the right image. With eight hours a day tied to the office, Joe decided to run ads. Interviewing distributor prospects would be a great way to utilize his time.

The Town Star Journal took Joe's ad.

HELP WANTED
Earn $300-500 a month part time.
Free training.
Unlimited potential for leaders.
999-9999

On Monday morning, the phone rang off the hook. There was a pent-up demand in Joe's town for well-paying part-time jobs. "I've hit the Mother Lode!" thought Joe after answering the 35th phone inquiry that morning.

After an exciting day of phone inquiries, Joe looked forward to Tuesday. "Fourteen appointments for interviews, and they are coming to see me! How hard can it possibly be to sponsor a prospect who comes to you? Maybe I should take a little time off to order my Mercedes."

Tuesday morning, the first appointment was waiting outside Joe's door.

"I'm here about the job in the paper. I assure you I'm the man you are looking for. I need work bad and can start right away."

Joe asked the young man to come into his office and began to explain the multilevel concept and the business opportunity. Joe went into detail about the products and the training. He explained how the young man could build a secure part-time business of his own with the unlimited opportunity marketing plan.

When Joe finished his presentation, there were two more prospects waiting by his door for their turns. The first young man said, "I'll think it over and call you tomorrow."

Joe invited the next two prospects into his office and began explaining his business opportunity.

After a few minutes, Joe realized he made a big mistake. Talking to two prospects at the same time was difficult. It was like a reverse *two-on-one*. And there were other distractions. The phone kept ringing with more inquiries from Joe's ad. Three of Joe's distributors stopped in to visit the new office and ask advice. An office equipment salesman stopped by to see if Joe needed a copier. And Joe's mother called to see how the new executive was doing.

Joe's two prospects lost interest and left. However, Joe didn't have to worry, he had eleven more appointments scheduled that day.

The rest of the day continued in the same manner. Some appointments didn't show up, and those that showed up, didn't join. Between all the interruptions, Joe did manage to set nine appointments for Tuesday morning.

Tuesday brought fewer interruptions. However, even with completely uninterrupted presentations, no one was sponsored into Joe's program. Joe thought, "Have I lost my presentation skills?"

On Wednesday, the office was very quiet. Joe spent the time planning his recruiting strategy and evaluating the previous two days' events. While his progress was disappointing, Joe saw that getting his presentation to masses of people was a positive step forward.

On Thursday, Joe had three interviews scheduled. Depression crept in when the first two didn't show up. The third appointment arrived late, but Joe gave him his best presentation. When Joe's prospect turned him down, Joe swallowed his pride and said, "I know this is a wonderful opportunity. Could you please tell me honestly why you aren't joining? I have talked to over fifteen people this week, and not one has signed up. I know you can't speak for all of them, but could you please tell me what is preventing you from becoming a distributor?"

Joe's prospect replied, "Joe, your opportunity sounds great. However, I don't need an opportunity. I need a *job*. I came here to earn money, not to spend money. With your program, I have to buy a distributor kit and invest in some starter products. That takes money out of my pocket. I need money *in* my pocket. I don't want unlimited opportunity. I want a part-time job to help pay my bills that are due this month."

Joe thanked his ex-prospect for his frank comments and wished him good luck in his job search.

"It's amazing that I couldn't see it!" thought Joe. "I can't believe I ran a help wanted ad. I attracted every unqualified prospect in town. On the bright side, at least my presentation skills aren't to blame. I'll re-run an ad next week, but I'll make sure it runs in the business opportunity section. At least I'll be making presentations to qualified prospects."

Sunday's paper ran the following ad:

BUSINESS OPPORTUNITY
Own your own part-time business. Major multilevel company looking for part-time distributors. Less than $100 to get started.
Call 999-9999

Monday was exciting. Although Joe received fewer ad responses, the quality was exceptional. The prospects calling were definitely looking for a low investment business opportunity, not a job. Joe had learned a lesson from last week: don't set too many appointments for one day. Interruptions can kill the presentation. Joe arranged four appointments each on Tuesday, Wednesday, and Thursday. He planned to arrange any additional appointments from ad responses for Friday.

Tuesday's first appointment was looking for an established business that he could take over and manage. He wasn't interested in direct marketing or building a sales business from scratch.

The second and third appointments said, "We're not interested in multilevel opportunities. We'd like something in manufacturing."

The last appointment didn't show up.

The rest of the week's appointments went the same. No new recruits, the prospects weren't interested.

Joe's patience was gone by Friday. He had to turn down some important *two-on-one* appointments with his downline because he had to cover the office. There were still a few scattered interviews. Joe could see his group regressing. Their enthusiasm was low and they missed their leader. In only two weeks time, his absence created lethargy in his once vibrant downline. "A leader must be out in the field setting an example for his group," thought Joe. "I'm hiding in an office doing something my group can't copy."

Friday's last appointment said, "I'm not interested."

Joe asked, "Before you leave, could you do me one favor? I've talked to several people this week about this business opportunity. Everyone turned me down. I can't understand it. Please be honest with me. I would really like to know the reason you turned down this opportunity."

Joe's prospect took a deep breath and began, "I came here looking for a part-time business opportunity that wouldn't require a large start-up investment. Joe, I really respect you. You are successful with this business opportunity and I would dearly love to be like you. However, you run your business out of a nice office. That would require quite an investment and commitment for me. You work full-time here and I can't quit my job. You invested in furniture, ads, etc. and I don't have that kind of capital. In order for me to be successful like you, I would have to do all those things. Joe, I can't afford to copy what you are doing to be successful."

Joe thanked his prospect for his frank appraisal and wished him a good weekend. Still in shock, Joe decided to take the weekend off. "I need to do some serious rethinking about this office project."

On Monday morning, Joe made his decision. He would terminate the office project. Joe had neglected his group, and the office project was an activity that new distributors couldn't copy. Multilevel is a business that succeeds when activities are duplicated and multiplied by one's downline. The office project didn't qualify.

"I need to talk to you," Joe said as he entered the building manager's office. "I've made a terrible mistake in leasing my office. I would like to know if I can break my lease."

After an hour's discussion, they reached a compromise. Joe couldn't break his lease, but the building management agreed to install a shower and a microwave in Joe's office. Joe could move out of his apartment and live in his office. At least Joe would be saving on apartment rent.

"Well, at least it's not all bad," thought Joe. "I'll have a prestigious address for my studio apartment."

Street Smarts don't pay off

Did you ever see a person with well-developed *street smarts*? The kind of person who is always on guard and afraid that someone is going to *do him in*? How easy is multilevel marketing for these skeptics?

Defensive, scared skeptics drive opportunity away. They look for the con, how another person is going to get them. They can't believe anyone would help them under any circumstance. Let's look at a typical example. The *street smart* prospect's thoughts are in parentheses.

Distributor: "Let me show you how Acme Corporation can give you an opportunity to make more money." (*Acme is a big corporation because they make money ripping off fools. I certainly won't fall for such an obvious con game.*)

Distributor: "Acme Corporation offers unlimited opportunity. They give you the chance to obtain financial freedom." (*Acme Corporation certainly has this guy brainwashed. I better watch my pockets. This guy seems sincere, but it might be a cover-up to trick me into believing him. Then he will get me big time.*)

Distributor: "I will help you every way I can. I'm dedicated to your success with Acme Corporation." (*Nobody offers to help without a price. This guy will get me in so he can make money off me while I earn nothing.*)

And so the conversation goes on. No matter how hard the distributor tries to help Mr. Street Smart, the resistance level of Mr. Street Smart never goes down. He does everything in his power to turn off, reject, and alienate himself from the opportunity offered. Because Mr. Street Smart is expecting the world to attack him, he counterattacks first. It doesn't matter if the person wants to help or to con Mr. Street Smart, his reaction is always the same — *attack!*

So what happens to good, legitimate, well-meaning people who come into contact with Mr. Street Smart? They avoid him. They don't need the grief from a scared, panic-stricken, paranoid skeptic. These good, well-meaning people spend their time with cooperative prospects who want help and opportunity.

Now for the bad news. If the *street smart* person drives away good, legitimate, well-meaning people, who's left for Mr. Street Smart to come in contact with? Only those people who wish to con, trick, deceive, cheat, and steal from Mr. Street Smart.

This verifies Mr. Street Smart's view of the world. Everyone he comes in contact with really does want to *do him in*. These are the only people attracted to him.

In Mr. Street Smart's world, everyone is out to get him. It is very difficult to spend 10 years of psychotherapy with Mr. Street Smart to change his attitude and view of the world. Let's leave this challenge to the professional head shrinkers. We should go on to locate prospects who want help and are ready, eager, and waiting for our opportunity.

"A chip on the shoulder comes from the block higher up."

Questions anyone?

"Never, never, never answer questions during opportunity meetings," said Big Al. "And if you are still in doubt, don't even think for a moment of answering a question."

Distributor Joe was puzzled. He thought, "After all my training and experience, why shouldn't I answer questions during opportunity meetings? Certainly many of the guests would have legitimate questions that would help them make a decision to join. Wouldn't it look funny if I refused to answer questions? I'd appear insecure or as if I was hiding something.

Big Al continued, "Now, I know you are thinking you are the hottest meeting giver in town. You feel that you are the expert on your company, and the most qualified person in the world to answer questions. However, let's look at our obligation to our guests. These are the people who gave up their valuable time to attend our meeting. What if we gave a meeting and allowed questions from the audience? Here are some problems."

1. If we start answering questions, our opportunity meeting becomes longer than our preplanned 30-40 minutes. If we have 20 new guests in the room, we could have 20 individual questions. In other words, the first guest may ask

a question that may be of a personal nature. The other 19 guests are bored as it doesn't pertain to them. The next guest may ask a technical question that applies to commercial accounts. After several of these questions, we've bored our guests and run our meeting overtime (the ultimate mistake).

2. One question leads to another. After bringing up one question, it sparks additional thoughts and questions from the guests. Soon you could be in a never-ending chain of related questions.

3. If we don't respect the time of our guests, they will penalize our insensitivity. They will refuse to evaluate our opportunity with an open mind. How positive would a guest be after 25 minutes of boring questions?

4. When we answer questions from guests, we start losing control of the meeting. There should always be someone in control, and it should be us. Our guests will appreciate the professionalism of a short, concise meeting that doesn't wander.

5. We want our distributors to begin opportunity meetings also. If they observe that we answer questions during meetings, they will refrain from starting their own meetings until they know all the answers.

6. What if a guest who's an expert in a certain field asks a technical question that you can't answer? Do you really need this embarrassment in front of your distributors and their guests?

7. Remember, this is an opportunity meeting, not a training meeting. We are here to give our guests a brief overview of the business. We don't teach every piece of data that we know about the business. We only wish to give enough facts so that our guests can make an intelligent decision. This is not the time to make our guests experts in our product lines, etc.

8. Finally, if our guests have questions of an individual nature, they should be answered **individually.** When a guest raises his hand to ask a question at my opportunity meetings, I politely reply, "I see there are questions. We appreciate your questions and we would like to answer each one individually. Please hold your questions for a few more minutes until we finish this meeting. We promise you that we will be over in just a bit. At that time we will sit down with each of you and explain further any details pertinent to your personal situation."

Distributor Joe was busy taking notes. "That makes a lot of sense. I never looked at it from the guests' viewpoint. It is unfair to turn the opportunity meeting into a training meeting. Most questions I have answered, are boring and run the meeting into overtime. Yet, I notice the smile on your face, Big Al. There's more to the story, isn't there?"

Big Al laughed and said, "In this world there are individuals who come to opportunity meetings for entertainment. They enjoy hearing themselves talk and get sadistic pleasure from embarrassing speakers. Maybe they are competitors, or just had a bad day at work. Whatever the reason, they certainly know how to ruin a meeting if we let them."

"All they have to do is ask one or two questions and that buries the speaker. There are some questions that no matter what you say, you dig yourself into a deeper hole."

"Joe, I know that you feel you are an expert. To prove this, let me ask you a few questions. Let's see if you can handle them without looking incompetent or embarrassed."

Distributor Joe liked the challenge. He knew he could answer almost anything. He even knew the viscosity coefficient of the molecular structure at minus 80 degrees Centigrade for each product. Certainly there couldn't be a question that would stump or embarrass him.

"Are you ready?" smiled Big Al. "Here comes question number one from your friendly guest sadist. Now remember, pretend that you are in front of a meeting room full of guests."

"Question one: Distributor Joe, I read in the paper that the company's founder is a crook, con man, and a child molester. Personally, none of this bothers me. However, if I get into this business and try to recruit people, what should I say to them? I know they will ask if the founder is going to rip them off again, and why is he allowed to start a new company while out on parole. I just don't know how I would answer that. What should I do? "

Distributor Joe squirmed. Blushing and stuttering, he replied, "Well, he really isn't all that bad. You know, well, the founder, well, don't believe everything you read, and uh, uh ..."

"Okay, maybe you are right, some questions are impossible to answer." Distributor Joe admitted. However, Big Al wasn't through with him yet.

"You know that many of the things asked or said are not true. However, the more we defend the truth in the meet-

ing, the more credibility we give to the inaccurate facts of the questioner. Let's try another one to further prove the point."

"Question two: Distributor Joe, my neighbor tried a bottle of your *Wonder Juice*. One hour after drinking some, she started cramping and developing severe stomach pains. They called the ambulance and took her to the hospital. The tests showed a definitive reaction to *Wonder Juice*. The hospital took out her spleen, kidneys, and amputated her left leg. The doctors said this reaction to *Wonder Juice* happens only once in every hundred or so cases. I use *Wonder Juice* myself, love it, and never had any severe reactions. Should we tell our customers of this potential reaction or just keep it a secret because it doesn't happen very often?"

Distributor Joe blushed, meekly nodded and said, "Okay, Big Al, you know no matter what I say I would dig myself into a bigger hole on this one. Obviously some people know how to ask just the right questions to ruin a meeting. Boy, if these questions were ever asked at my meeting, I would be in real trouble. Now I understand why you were smiling. This one reason alone outweighs the other eight reasons combined. I'm cured, no more questions at my opportunity meetings."

Big Al added, "It is hard enough to give a meeting without the burden of preparing answers for questions that could come up. If you want to hear something really sad, just think of this situation. A new distributor is giving a meeting and is very nervous. All of a sudden he forgets what to say next or has run out of things to say. When a nervous speaker gets in this situation, what does he normally say?"

"Oh, no," groaned Distributor Joe. "Whenever a nervous speaker can't think of anything to say, he usually falls back on the old standby '*Are there any questions?*' The nervous speaker feels that letting the audience ask questions gives him time to think and regroup. That's jumping from the frying pan into the fire!"

"I'm glad we had this discussion," offered Distributor Joe. "The next time someone raises his hand to ask a question, you're guaranteed I won't be taking his question."

So you just have to run that ad

One day you sit at home wondering who you can get into your multilevel business. You have already contacted your personal list of prospects. Now you are forced to find new people.

Then, the world's greatest idea hits you. "Wouldn't it be great if prospects came to me? I could sit back, pick and choose from distributor prospects. I'll run an ad!"

On Friday, you tell your employer that you won't be in next week. (You say it's vacation time. However, you know next week will send you on to financial freedom. You'll never have to go back. Such is the power of the ad you plan to run in Sunday's paper.)

On Monday morning the phone rings nonstop from the special Help Wanted Ad you placed. It is exciting to talk with so many people looking for opportunity. Yet, at the end of the day, the excitement has died. You didn't make a single recruiting appointment. All talk, but no results. What went wrong?

After a careful review of the day's phone calls, a pattern

of misfortune becomes clear. The problems could be summed up as follows:

1. Too many unqualified *salary seekers*. Sure they're looking for an opportunity, but only a *guaranteed* one. Their response? "Why, I could work for weeks and not earn anything!"

2. The *free riders* want to know the benefit package details — "How much vacation do I get?" (Sounds like a real dedicated worker.) If there aren't full health, dental and disability programs, they just won't bother.

3. "Where is your office? Certainly you aren't serious about interviewing me at some coffee shop. I am looking for a respectable job."

4. "I have to *pay* for a kit to get started? I want to earn money, not spend money. And I have to buy products too? Are you for real?"

5. "Tell me about the job over the phone. I have twenty ads circled here and I am trying to sort out which ones I should see." The prospect is looking for a reason to eliminate you from his list.

6. "I am sorry. I won't give you my name and phone number. Some salesman might call. Don't call me, I'll call you."

Certainly, Help Wanted ads may draw some unqualified people. What about a Help Wanted Part-Time ad? The same problems could occur. Again we are *tied down, babysitting* the phone when other activities could be more productive.

On the positive side, a Help Wanted Part-Time ad could draw *employed* individuals. They look for ways to supplement their incomes instead of seeking survival income. At least these prospects have a base income and could wait while their business develops income. The question is, "How many employed individuals in your area read Help Wanted ads?"

What about a Business Opportunity ad? Fewer readers make the response rate low, but the callers are more qualified. These readers are not looking for a dead-end salary.

What are they looking for? Most want an established business that they can buy. Their opening questions are, "How many established accounts are in place?" or "What are the present gross sales and profits?" Most business opportunity seekers want to *buy* success, not *build* from the ground floor in a multilevel opportunity.

So, are all ads bad?

No. Every recruiting method has some good features. In the next chapter, let's look at one technique that overcomes many of the problems that can arise from placing newspaper ads.

One possible solution

Don't want to be tied down answering the phone?

Want to increase the number of responses to your ad?

Would you like to get your message across without interruption and questions?

And finally, wouldn't it be great to spend your time with pre-qualified prospects interested in your opportunity?

When your ad says, "Call for a recorded message," you can accomplish the above goals. Let's look at a sample ad and how a prospect would react after reading the ad in his Sunday newspaper.

ATTENTION MLM'ERS
If you are serious about your career, call for this important recorded message.
999-9999

Pete Prospect reads the ad and thinks, "It's just a recorded message. I can call right now while my interest is high. I won't have to wait until Monday morning. It sounds pretty non-threatening. I am usually afraid to call ads. There is always an amphetamine-crazed salesman on the other end trying to pressure me into an interview. They never want to give you any information. They insist you come in before they will tell you anything. This sounds pretty neat. I can call, listen to the information, and if I'm not interested, I'll hang up. It won't waste my time or theirs. I'm curious what it is all about. Let me call right now."

When Pete Prospect calls, he will receive a two or three minute recording. The message will answer his basic questions and qualify his prospect status. A sample recording could go like this:

"Thanks for calling. In the next 2 1/2 minutes I would like to tell you about an opportunity to increase your multilevel income. If you've been in multilevel marketing, you know how hard it is to build a large, successful distributor group and earn good money.

You may be representing a fine company, with a fine product, and with a great marketing bonus plan that pays great percentages. However, none of these factors will make you money unless you have a large, successful distributor group.

Believe me, I know how frustrating it can be. I worked hard for three years in multilevel before someone showed me the secret to multilevel success.

Want to know the secret?

A unique, high powered, training workshop that rockets distributors to the top. A training workshop that keeps distributors excited, productive, and earning big money.

How did I find out about this workshop?

Six months ago, I was working very hard in my multi-level program and making no money. I answered a similar ad and ACME Corporation invited me to a meeting. At the meeting, I saw that ACME was a good company (but my present company was pretty good, too). I saw that ACME had great products (but my present company had great products, too). ACME had a good bonus program (but so did my my present company).

The difference? Their distributors were making big money. When I asked why, I found the secret to multilevel marketing success: The ACME Corporation Distributor Transformation Training Program. Every distributor raved about how this unique training made them successful. Many people were former unsuccessful multilevel distributors like me.

My reaction?

I liked my present company, but I knew I was in multi level to make money. I figured, 'What do I have to lose?'

I checked out the ACME Distributor Transformation Training Program. Not only did it change my income potential, but I saw how this training would transform my new distributors into earning, excited distributors."

The last six months have been the most successful in my life. And the next six months can be just as exciting for you!

If you're looking for success in multilevel marketing, I urge you to get more information about this wonderful opportunity.

I'll be glad to send you literature including a free cassette tape explaining more about ACME and ACME's Distributor Transformation Training Program. You can review it in your own home with no obligation. If you want the information mailed to you, please leave your name and address at the end of this message. If you want to talk to someone in person and ask additional questions, leave your phone number and I will call you back.

Again, thanks so much for calling. You'll be excited when you receive this valuable information.

At the beep you may leave your name, address, or phone number if you prefer."

Would you leave you name and address to get additional information? Probably.

This is a sample ad that is targeted to present multilevel distributors. The ad may be completely different if your company's major selling point was a unique product or exciting car program. However, let's look at the recruiting principles used in this recorded message technique.

1. Your ad works 24 hours a day. People can call anytime, day or night. When people wait until the next day, a large percentage will forget.

2. You're not tied down to the phone. There is nothing worse than putting your business on hold while you wait and worry you might miss a phone call.

3. You'll receive more responses when people can call without fear of high pressure. What can be safer than calling a recorded message? You can now tap the *shy people* market. They can make good multilevel distributors too.

4. People know they will be listening to a recorder. Because you pre-warned them in your ad, you won't have problems with people who hate electronic answering machines.

5. This is a terrific way to save time by *presorting* prospects. Someone married to his present opportunity will hang up. Curiosity seekers will hang up when the message is over. Total multilevel *burnouts* will hang up. Only real prospects will leave their names for follow-up.

6. The recording gets your message across without interruption. You don't have control problems with the prospect asking questions out of sequence.

7. It is a low pressure, professional way to inform people of your opportunity.

8. You are in control. Not the prospect. You are dictating the opportunity and eventual interview on your terms. (How can a prospect argue and compete with a recording?)

This all sounds good, but what about the cost?

The ad is short and inexpensive. You do all your selling on the recording, not in expensive advertising space.

A good recording machine that handles two to three minute outgoing messages costs less than $100. And you can always use it personally when your ad stops running.

The literature and cassette are inexpensive. (Most cassette tapes cost about 60 cents each.) The total cost of your mailing package will be about $1.50 or $2.00. That's not much to pay for a good prospect. Think of the money you will save on gas. Plus, you won't have to buy your prospect a cup of coffee at some restaurant. Finally, many people will leave their phone number for instant information. These people don't require a mailing package. You can answer their questions over the phone and invite them directly to an opportunity meeting.

THE FOLLOW-UP

This is the easiest part. Instead of trying to explain abstract, complex principles over the phone, your prospect has already received this information for review. He has read it, and now you can talk intelligently about these facts.

If there is a real interest on his part, invite him to an opportunity meeting. Or, you can set a *two-on-one* appointment at his convenience.

To start the follow-up process, you will have to take the initiative. Most prospects won't have the initiative to call you. You will have to call them.

Where do you get their phone number if they only left their name and address? Simply look it up in the phone book or call directory assistance. If their number is unlisted, send a postcard urging them to call about additional information you forgot to send.

In summation, is this the only way to run an ad?

No, but many of the principles here can be a valuable addition to your newspaper ad campaign.

Dear Gabby

Dear Gabby,

I am a 30 year old man with a problem. Since I was 10 years old, I have always been afraid of women. In school, I was petrified to attend classes with female students and female teachers. I dreaded the thought of returning home because my mother was female. Even today, everywhere I look, I see women.

I desperately wish to get married, but my fears have kept me from approaching women to ask for dates. This may not seem like a big problem to you, but I really need help and advice. Please, please, answer my letter.

Sincerely,

Scared & Small Minded

Dear Scared and Small Minded,

You are the most disgusting wimp that has ever written me. I have never in my life read such a ridiculous, petty, and immature letter. Why don't you be like most people? Become self-confident, self-sufficient and stop living with your minuscule, baby problems. We positive thinkers think big and consider people like you to be the lowest form of human life. Why don't you take your crayons and write your letters to someone else? We normal people don't have time for you.

With disgust,

Gabby

With responses like the above, how many letters do you think Gabby will get in the future? Few, if any. When people are put down, they stay away from any situation that may give a repeat performance. People avoid embarrassment like a plague.

What happens to the observers who were not put down by Gabby? They also avoid contact with Gabby. They don't want to be next.

How does this apply to multilevel leaders and recruiters? Have you ever had a distributor or prospect ask you an absolutely dumb, negative, and silly question? How did you respond? Did you shrug it off as not worthy of an answer? Did you give a quick and condescending answer? Did you make fun of his stupidity? Or, did you destroy the question and the questioner to impress any observers?

These reactions drive away not only the prospect, but distributors as well.

Many leaders get so positive and hyped about their opportunities that they overwhelm any negative input or questions. While it is nice to be positive, too much adrenaline is dangerous. Let's put ourselves in a sample situation to see how our reaction to dumb questions can affect the prospect's decision to join.

You are doing a *two-on-one* presentation with a brand new distributor. Halfway through the presentation your prospect asks, "Is this a pyramid? Just where does all this money go? The people who start at the top? Is this some kind of a rip-off?"

You answer, "Any fool paying attention can see these bonuses come from middleman profits in the retail distribution method. Everyone knows pyramids are illegal. I'm surprised you would even ask that dumb question. It's obvious you don't understand business, so please pay attention while I explain the rest of our opportunity!"

What do you think is going through the prospect's mind? Would he think, "If I ask another question, this guy will carve his initials on my forehead. Working with him would destroy this opportunity for me. I'd better be quiet and let him finish and hope he goes away."

What's going on in your new distributor's mind? Would he think, "Looks like my sponsor has blown my prospect. I'd better apologize to my prospect after my sponsor leaves. I won't ask my sponsor any questions or try to learn anything from him. He may react the same way with me. When this presentation is over, I'll call my other appointments and cancel them. I don't want my sponsor to blow them away also."

Well, if this is not the way to answer stupid questions, how should they be handled? First, we must understand why prospects ask stupid questions.

Prospects put us under the microscope and judge us more than they judge the opportunity. When they ask a question, they are doing it for several reasons:

1. We go too fast or assume too much. Just because we know all about multi-level marketing, we shouldn't assume that our prospects have the same insights. Our prospects are really asking us the question, "This is very interesting. Because I find it interesting, I wish more information or some clarification on this point."

2. The prospect wants to see how we operate under pressure. They want a leader who is calm and composed. They want confidence in their upline.

3. The prospect is interested in his own problems. If you ignore or downplay his problems, the prospect feels you won't care enough to help him succeed.

With this in mind, what if our answer to the profits and pyramid questions was this: "That's a good question. I wondered that myself when I first looked at this opportunity. When I attended the company training workshops, they explained how our bonuses were a redistribution of the normal middleman profits. Instead of the middleman getting all the money, we did the same work and received the profit instead. The harder we work, the higher up the ladder of management we can climb. Our company has a pyramid structure just like General Motors. We can move up the ladder of success based on our efforts."

Isn't this answer a little different now that we understand *why* our prospect is asking questions? Our reactions to stupid questions can make a big difference in our recruiting efforts. Let's keep our prospects and new distributors saying, "My upline is interested in me and my questions and problems. I want to work with somebody like that."

The best people

Who are the best potential leaders for your MLM business? What characteristics give the potential leaders the edge?

Of course, we as MLM professionals would never prejudge an individual. However, we certainly can enhance our progress if we can isolate success characteristics of the great leaders in MLM. Let's do a little exercise that can help us isolate those needed characteristics.

Imagine the perfect stereotype MLM leader. What profession would he be in? An engineer? An accountant? A salesman? A business owner? In what order would you put the chosen professions? Take a minute or two and write on a separate sheet of paper which stereotype profession would produce the best MLM leaders.

Now, let's look at the number one duty of successful MLM leaders. TRAINING. If we are to duplicate ourselves, we must become effective trainers. This is the key to building large and successful organizations.

So who are the greatest trainers? TEACHERS! Teachers have honed their training skills daily to become the preferred profession of MLM recruiters. What do new downline distributors want? A patient, skilled, concerned trainer. Doesn't that describe a teacher?

And teachers are notoriously underpaid! They appreciate the opportunity of being fairly compensated for their skills. A multilevel opportunity can give them the cash flow needed to continue in their chosen profession.

Who are the best teachers? Band teachers. Not only do they have the patience and training skills of the teaching profession, they also have great promotional skills. They systematically raise money for band instruments, uniforms and trips. They have the sales ability of the greatest salesman mixed with the training professionalism of the teacher. This is a perfect combination for the true multilevel leader.

After teachers, then what? How about housewives? They also have great patience (they put up with husbands) and excellent training skills. Not only are they experienced trainers with their children, but many times they have to completely retrain their husbands.

And housewives are notoriously underpaid! They would love to have an extra income they could call their own, an income they could spend as they please. Plus, this is their chance to prove their real value. Many times they outearn their husbands after a few months of business building.

Housewives have the perfect skills for managing their MLM business. Cash flow and cash management experience from constantly restricted budgets. They are pros at making a little money go a long way. Inventory control experience from years of handling food and clothing needs. Time management experience from keeping track of five or six different schedules in their households. Plus, overall management and motivational skills to keep the family happy. Most Harvard MBAs don't have a fraction of the average housewives' management skills.

Now, what about salesmen? How do they rank?

What is the stereotype image of the average salesman? A hustler or peddler who pressures a customer into buying something he doesn't need. Then, the salesman quickly runs on to the next prospect while leaving his original customer orphaned forever. All that interests the stereotype salesman is how to make the next sale with someone new. Avoid follow-up and service. Does this sound like your multilevel leader profile?

The stereotype salesman has just the opposite skills needed to be an effective and successful MLM leader! New distributors need follow-up, patience and training. They don't need an absent leader.

When people ask you if you have to be a salesman to be a successful MLM leader, you can answer, "Only if you want to start with a handicap."

So, look for your potential leaders from individuals who have the patience to train their groups. Of course, there are good salesmen and bad salesmen, good teachers and bad teachers. Don't just look in certain professions, but look for the characteristics that make successful MLM leaders.

Booths, trade shows, and fairs

Wouldn't it be nice if all we had to do to recruit new distributors was to open a booth? People could walk by, stop and look at our opportunity. They would sponsor and order many products. We would never have to prospect again. People would just beat a path to our door.

So much for dreaming. Let's get back to reality since our monthly bonus checks are based on production. However, is there a way to make booths, trade shows, and fairs a productive prospecting tool? Let's examine the typical trade show booth.

Joe Distributor hears about a wonderful multilevel trade show in a large city. Thousands of prospective multilevel prospects will come to the show looking for an opportunity. Joe Distributor says to himself, "All I have to do is to rent a booth, and my recruiting troubles will be over."

Joe then sends in his deposit of $300 or $400 for his booth. Next, he makes up some banners to project a professional appearance. Cost: $200. With 4,000 prospects expected, Joe orders some literature from the home office. For mini catalogs, applications, order forms, marketing explanations, etc., Joe's total cost is $600.

The budget for air fare, hotel accommodations, food, etc. is $800. Since Joe's cash investment is pretty high already, he decides to attend the trade show alone. It would be too expensive to bring along a distributor to assist him.

With a total investment of $2,000 , Joe expects big things from his trade show venture. If only 1% of the projected visitors join, Joe would have 40 (4,000 attending times 1%) brand new distributors in his group! Imagine getting 40 brand new distributors in one weekend! That's exciting!

The big weekend arrives and Joe sets up his booth early. As the show opens, Joe prepares to give out his brochure pack to the first individual who walks by. A prospect strolls by Joe's booth and continues walking without even stopping to look. Several more prospects walk by without even acknowledging Joe's existence. Something must be wrong so Joe takes a hard look at his booth.

"Aha!" thinks Joe. "So that's the key. I must move my booth out into the aisle slightly so people will have to make a detour to get around it. That will make them notice."

Sure enough, someone noticed. Unfortunately it was the trade show director. He politely asks Joe to move his booth out of the traffic flow.

Finally, a prospect stops at Joe's booth. "Just give me some free literature to look over. I don't have much time. There are 50 other booths for me to visit." Grabbing a handful of literature, Joe's first prospect quickly disappears into the next aisle.

The next prospect said, "Why don't you have flashier free literature packages like booth #46? And where are your free samples?"

The booth next to Joe's asked for several brochures so they could compare their program to Joe's. Then they used Joe's literature for comparison to entice prospects into their program.

With no luck, Joe decided to have lunch. He quickly grabbed a sandwich and a soft drink. He returned to find that half of his brochures were missing from his display. "Well, at least somebody got information about my program. I had trouble just giving it away!" thought Joe.

The afternoon was as bad as the morning. Joe tried to present his opportunity to several prospects, but they didn't have time to sit through a 25 minute presentation. At other times, Joe would give a presentation only to be interrupted by brochure collectors.

Joe thought he had one good prospect who seemed extremely interested. However, at the end of the presentation his prospect said he was in 11 other multilevel programs. He thought Joe's program might make it an "even dozen."

"Just what I need," mumbled Joe, "A multilevel junkie that can only put 5% of his time into my program. Plus, he will try to move all my distributors to his other 11 programs. Headaches like that I don't need!"

By the end of the day, Joe had classified the passing attendees into three categories.

1. The brochure collectors. They had nothing else to do that day so they came to collect brochures. They hoped to get some good ideas for their programs. You could spot them easily by the sacks they carried. Some even brought backpacks and wagons. They were the ones who always asked for samples of your product.

2. The multilevel junkies. They were looking for the latest program to join. These individuals were easily spotted by filling out applications for any program that had no sign-up cost. They didn't have any money to spend for products, etc. They were still investing in start-up costs for their other 11 companies. At least Joe was smart enough to avoid getting them into his program.

3. The proselytizers. These people were already multilevel distributors who came to recruit every booth into their present program. They reasoned that if someone invested in a booth, he should be a good prospect to get into their program. And there were 50 booths at the show, so they could approach 50 prospects without personally investing in a booth. They had no luck as the booth owners were interested in promoting their own program to recoup their $2,000 investment.

The day ended with Joe having dinner with some of the other booth owners. The conversation was negative.

"I didn't get one good solid lead for my program."

"I wish the trade show visitors had more of a work ethic. They just wanted something for nothing."

"I'm out of literature already, and I couldn't get people to leave their names and phone numbers for future follow-up."

"The trade show promoter told me only 600 people showed up today. I was expecting 2,000 per day for both days. I don't think we are going to have the 4,000 people projected by the trade show promoter."

"I went to lunch and someone stole my briefcase, sports coat, and brochure rack from my booth."

Joe was getting depressed. He had counted on getting 1% of 4,000 people to join his program. With his total outlay of $2,000 in expenses, it would have cost him $50 per distributor ($2,000 expenses divided by 40 new distributors). If only 1,200 people showed up, 1% sign-ups would only be 12 distributors! The net cost per distributor then would be $166! Ouch!

At a new distributor cost of $50, Joe felt he could do better by bribing people to join instead of buying a booth in the trade show. But, since he already paid for the booth, he reasoned that the trade show would be good experience. "Maybe it will put me in contact with a whole new group of people," thought Joe.

"Yet, if the new distributor cost soars to $166 with fewer people showing up for the show, I know I could spend the money more efficiently elsewhere. Heck, even my negative, worthless brother-in-law would join for $166!"

All this depended on getting 12 new distributors. Joe hadn't sponsored his first distributor yet, and the trade show had only one more day to run. Joe was pinning big hopes on tomorrow.

The next day brought good news and bad news. The bad news was that only 300 prospects showed up at the trade show. The good news was that each booth owner had more time to talk with each prospect.

Joe did sign up one distributor, so the day was not a total failure. However, Joe's new distributor was new to multi-level marketing and was going to need plenty of help. Joe figured it would take several weeks of *two-on-ones* to give him a decent start. More bad news. His new distributor lived locally, and that was about 900 miles from Joe's home town. Things were definitely going from bad to worse.

Joe returned home the next day with one new distributor application. This included a commitment to travel 900 miles to help his new distributor. This was the most expensive distributor Joe ever sponsored. If Joe continued doing trade shows and recruiting distributors at a net cost of $2,000 each, he could afford to be in business for about four more weeks.

This episode wasn't going to make Joe's career highlight films.

"Hmmm. Maybe I should call Big Al? I still have a quarter."

The secret ingredients

"Let's go to this small trade show right here in town," explained Big Al. "That will remove the travel and hotel expense right away. Remember, we are in multilevel to make a profit."

"I don't use trade shows for recruiting myself. However, I'll go with you this time to show you how to maximize your recruiting and minimize your expenses. You have to outsmart the other trade show booths to get your share of the good prospects. You can use the same banner and we will need only $100 worth of literature. We will be very selective about deciding who receives it."

"Don't worry about a thing. I will bring my **two secret ingredients** and we will have fun and a profitable time."

Distributor Joe's excitement was building. Big Al was going to help him recoup his losses from the last trade show disaster. Only 1,000 people were expected at this trade show, but Distributor Joe knew Big Al wouldn't let him down. The total cost of this show was:

$150	Booth
100	Literature
50	Food
50	Miscellaneous supplies
$350	**Total expenditures**

With the banner already paid for, and no large travel expenses, this show was already shaping up as a profitable venture.

Joe and Big Al arrived at 8:00 AM to arrange their booth. And was Joe ever surprised to see Big Al's two secret ingredients!

1. Big Al's computer and printer

2. A fish bowl with a couple hundred 3x5 index cards

Big Al said, "Joe, at most trade shows you have a lot of unqualified brochure collectors, multilevel junkies, and proselytizers. However, you also have some very good prospects. What are the two biggest challenges in reaching these qualified prospects?"

Joe replied, "My two biggest problems are:

1. Getting prospects to stop at my booth. I really need something to attract them. There are so many booths, all alike. The prospects just walk through in a daze, not stopping at any of them.

2. Getting the prospects to leave their names and phone numbers for future follow-up. If I don't get the names and phone numbers, I'm wasting my time.

Are you suggesting your two secret ingredients will solve these problems?"

Big Al laughed and said, "Just watch what happens when the prospects come in. Let's put up this poster and watch the prospects flock to our table."

Joe helped Big Al fasten the poster above their display. The poster said:

Test Your
Multi-Level
I.Q.

$100 Of Product To The Winner!

Before they securely fastened the poster, two prospects sneaked in early. They said to Big Al, "Let us try this Multilevel I.Q. Test. We want to see which one of us scores the highest. The loser buys lunch."

Big Al sat the first prospect down in front of the computer. The computer was flashing enticing graphics that was already drawing a crowd. Big Al explained, "This is a multiple choice, 20 question test. When you make your choice, enter A, B or C. The computer will automatically go on to the next question. When you are through, the computer will print out your score and a brief commentary concerning your abilities."

The prospect rubbed his hands together and said, "Let's go. I'm ready to prove my expertise."

A few more prospects gathered around to watch.

The 20 questions on Big Al's computer were:

1. What product line is most conducive to multilevel marketing?
(A) Unique products
(B) Consumable products
(C) High tech products

2. What is the average sales volume of the average multilevel distributor?
(A) $60
(B) $100
(C) $150 or more.

3. What method builds retail business fastest?
(A) Direct Mail
(B) Telemarketing
(C) Advertising

4. When is the best time to get referrals?
(A) Just after signing up
(B) After a successful experience
(C) When turned down

5. What product line accounts for the majority of multilevel sales volume in America?
(A) Cleaners
(B) Vitamins
(C) Cosmetics

6. Which profession statistically makes the most successful multilevel distributor?
(A) Business owners
(B) Housewives
(C) Salesmen

7. Which advertising medium has the best success ratio for recruiting?
(A) Newspaper
(B) Radio
(C) Direct Mail

8. What is the number one concern of new distributors?
(A) Product pricing
(B) Recruiting leads
(C) Training

9. Which premium motivates multilevel distributors most?
(A) Car
(B) Travel
(C) Cash

10. Which common retailing contest gets the best results?
(A) Bucket Brigade
(B) Coupon Royale
(C) Punchcard Madness

11. Which recruiting technique automatically closes undecided and uninterested prospects?
(A) Bathroom trick
(B) Reasons why
(C) Reasons why not

12. What test is used to identify leaders instantly?
(A) Eagle test
(B) Home office letter
(C) Oyster warming

13. What is the ideal length of an opportunity meeting?
(A) 30 minutes
(B) 1 hour
(C) 90 minutes

14. What night of the week will get the best opportunity meeting attendance?
(A) Monday
(B) Tuesday
(C) Thursday

15. What close sells burned-out distributors?
(A) Training
(B) Product
(C) Money

16. What ad answering technique gives the best control and results for recruiting?
(A) Answering machine
(B) Answering service
(C) Live

17. What type of meeting will keep your distributors motivated longer?
(A) Motivational
(B) Family
(C) Instructional

18. What is the most important factor in choosing a multilevel company?
(A) Product line
(B) Marketing program
(C) Management

19. What percentage increase in income do new distributors receive when finishing a comprehensive multilevel business building workshop?
(A) 50%
(B) 100%
(C) 150% or more

20. What factor keeps hard-working distributors from earning the big money in multilevel marketing?
(A) Lack of upline support
(B) Lack of training availability
(C) The company they represent.

As soon as the first prospect answered question #20, the printer immediately started printing the following:

```
YOUR SCORE:  45%

YOUR PRESENT MULTILEVEL ABILITIES RANK YOU IN
THE BOTTOM 33% OF ALL DISTRIBUTORS.

FURTHER TRAINING AND STUDYING
HIGHLY RECOMMENDED

PROGNOSIS FOR FUTURE SUCCESS IN MULTILEVEL:
SEMI-DISMAL UNLESS HELP IS ACQUIRED

UNDERSTANDING OF BUSINESS:  INADEQUATE

NEED FOR PROFESSIONAL SPONSOR:  IMMENSE

BY THE WAY, YOU HAVE A NICE KEYBOARD TOUCH!
```

Everyone watching had a big laugh. The prospect's friend quickly sat down to take his test. The rest of the crowd lined up for their opportunity to take their test. They couldn't wait to see how they ranked. The crowd grew larger as more prospects gathered around wondering what was the big attraction.

Distributor Joe whispered to Big Al, "I see what you mean. This really does solve my #1 problem, getting people attracted to my booth. I am going to have everyone attending here. This is great! People can't resist the chance to test their recruiting I.Q. I won't have to stand in the middle of the aisle to drag people to my booth. This is terrific! We definitely outsmarted the rest of the exhibitors. They have "me too" booths and we have the best attraction around."

The first prospect turned to Big Al and said, "That test was super interesting. Can I get the answers to the questions? You folks sure seem to know a lot about multilevel marketing. Also, I just need to know about those retailing contests. What is the Coupon Royale? There are so many things in this test I haven't heard of, but I really need to know. When can we sit down and talk?"

Big Al said they were busy until the show closed at 6:00 PM. However, he would be happy to meet him for lunch or immediately after the show. The prospect eagerly set an appointment and said, "Will you bring me the answers to the test?"

Big Al said, "We only have so many sets of answers. If you fill out this 3x5 card with your name, address, and phone number — we'll gladly send you a copy. We'll also include some other materials you will find interesting. Plus, if you have the highest score, you win $100 worth of products. Just put your score on the back of the card."

The prospect thanked Big Al and said, "I'm looking forward to our meeting this evening." Distributor Joe smiled when Big Al dropped the first card into the fish bowl. That solves problem #2 — how to get prospects' names and phone numbers.

Big Al and Distributor Joe didn't have time for lunch. The response to their Multilevel I.Q. Test was overwhelming. They quickly filled their evening with *two-on-one* appointments.

Big Al and Joe sponsored 100% of their appointments that evening. It was so easy. The prospects were in awe of these two experts who knew the answers to making multilevel marketing work. Plus, Big Al used the *stair step* technique to the fullest. Every prospect wanted to sign right away because they knew the next prospects would be in their downline. This display of good recruiting techniques motivated Joe. Joe was watching a *recruiting explosion*.

After the last two-on-one appointment, Big Al analyzed the basic points for Distributor Joe.

1. The cost was low because they were local. Travel and lodging expenses add to the cost of a booth. It is a formidable overhead that can put you out of business.

2. Most leads from local shows are local. This means substantial dollar savings when you work with your new distributors.

3. The challenge of a competitive test draws prospects to you. You don't have to be a carnival huckster trying to pull people out of the aisles.

4. The computer display costs only a few sheets of printer paper. This is a lot cheaper than giving fancy brochures to freeloaders.

5. The prize and excitement of the test draws a crowd at your booth. This crowd attracts an even larger crowd.

6. The prize makes it easy to get their names, addresses and phone numbers for easy follow-up.

7. With the prospects you don't recruit, you can sell the names, addresses and phone numbers to mailing list brokers. This further reduces the net cost of your booth.

8. The Multilevel I.Q. Test sets you apart from the other booths because it establishes you as an *expert*. Participants want to know the answers to their tests. Everyone wants to make an appointment with the expert. This makes *two-on-one* appointments a snap.

9. By incorporating the *stair step* recruiting technique, you can sign up prospects immediately. You don't have to worry about procrastination. One good trade show could produce a chain of distributors 50 levels deep. Just think what that could do to your product volume.

This was a two day trade show so Big Al arranged for one of Distributor Joe's first level distributors to work the second day. Joe was a quick learner, so there was no need for Big Al to stick around. Now, Joe could train one of his distributors in the fine art of recruiting at trade shows.

Test answers

1. (B)

Unique and high-tech products require more salesmanship. If 95% of the population are "non-sales" types, you would be excluding this large segment from your opportunity. Fortunately, if a distributor can't sell, he can at least consume. Your bonus check is based on volume.

2. (A)

Everyone (companies, sponsors, distributors) wishes the average was higher.

3. (C)

All three methods can work. However, direct mail requires additional skills and a higher capital expenditure. Telemarketing requires a masochistic desire for rejection.

4. (B)

Anytime is a good time to get referrals, but it is *so easy* after a successful experience.

5. (B)

A vitamin or food supplement program can easily cost $50 a month. That's a lot of cleaners or face creams.

6. (B)

Housewives have more skills.

7. (C)

An advertisement in the newspaper or on the radio reaches the general population. Unfortunately, only a small percentage of the general population cares about a part-time opportunity. With direct mail, you can better target your prospect.

8. (C)

Available training boosts a new distributor's self-confidence. No matter how good the product pricing, or how many leads are available, if the distributor feels unqualified to try, nothing happens.

9. (A)

Cash is quickly spent and forgotten. Travel lasts but a few days. A car is an everyday reminder of the benefits of multilevel marketing.

10. (D)

Hey, if the prospect got *all* the answers right, they wouldn't need to talk with you. Of course this is unfair — but this is *war*.

11. (A)

This technique only works during a *two-on-one* presentation. Reasons why and why not are logical. Logic doesn't sell, emotion and credibility sells.

12. (A)

This one is too easy. Have you ever heard of someone getting motivated from a letter from the home office? Anyway, if you waited several weeks for a letter from the home office to determine your leaders, you've waited too long. Oyster warming will determine if a new distributor is dealing with unqualified prospects.

13. (A)

The only person who likes long opportunity meetings is the speaker, and he is already a distributor. You want the opportunity meetings to be short so you'll have time to sponsor your prospect and answer his questions.

14. (B)

There's Monday Night Football. Enough said. Thursday is almost the weekend. You certainly wouldn't want to interfere with a prospect's "free time."

15. (A)

A new technique or method can be a new lease on life.

16. (A)

"Live" voices can answer questions. Many prospects sort through ads by looking for reasons not to join. If they can't ask disqualifying questions, they can't disqualify your opportunity until you call them back. Then, you at least have their phone number and can control the conversation.

17. (B)

A *rah-rah*, hype, motivational meeting wears off in a day or two. Instructional meetings are like going to school. But family meetings (pot luck dinners, activities, etc.) bonds your distributors beyond just the money opportunity.

18. (C)

Good management can always bring in a new product line or change the marketing program. A marketing plan or a product line cannot bring in good management.

19. (C)

New distributors earn little bonus. Any increase would be substantial.

20. (B)

Hard-working distributors who don't earn big money aren't working the business properly. Instead of correcting their mistakes through repetition and hard work, training could give them new, proven methods for increasing their earnings.

How to get the best out of your speakers

Most people hate introducing a speaker. Why? Because it is difficult to make a concise, motivating, and professional introduction. That is, **unless** you have a formula.

What happens when you trash a speaker's introduction? He has to crawl out of an eight-foot hole just to get the audience's positive reception. Let's take an example of a bad introduction and how it affects the distributors' and prospects' attention.

"Ladies and gentlemen. Thank you so much for coming out this evening. I know we have a small crowd, but most people stayed at home to watch the ball game this evening. My name is John Boring and I am a distributor for Acme Corporation. I started about 3 months ago and now my wife is getting involved also. My wife couldn't be here tonight because one of our children has the flu. She will probably be here next week. There is a lot of the flu bug going around. Maybe that is why many people couldn't make it here this evening. I know we aren't starting on time. We are waiting for a few more people to show up, but we are going to get started now. I don't know how long our speaker will talk tonight, but we will probably run a little late. I am not going

to be speaking, so let me introduce our speaker for tonight. Oh, by the way, we will have refreshments at the back after the meeting.

Tonight we invited Mr. Big Time, President of Acme Corporation, to speak to us. Unfortunately, due to business scheduling difficulties, he couldn't make it. So we invited Mr. Almost Big, the Vice President of Acme Corporation, but he refused to come. That left us with our old standby, my sponsor, Jim Goodheart. We all know that Jim is an exciting speaker. However, he cannot be with us this evening as he hasn't shown up. So, anyway, Sam Nobody is going to speak, and uh, uh, we'll go ahead now. So, here's Sam."

Sam Nobody humbly shuffles to the front of the room. Poor Sam. No credibility, no respect, no applause. The audience was dissapointed with this *substitute* speaker and they showed it. No mercy for Sam. Let him squirm. The audience yawned, shuffled, and talked throughout Sam's presentation.

Well, we can't blame it all on John Doe who introduced Sam Nobody. Sam should have prepared John with an outline of how to introduce him. Or, in the absence of an outline, maybe John could have used the *T.I.P.* formula for error-free, perfect introductions.

What is the *T.I.P.* formula?

T stands for topic. A brief description of tonight's meeting and discussion.

I stands for importance. Why the topic is of importance and interest to our audience.

P stands for person. A short background of credentials which qualify this person to be our speaker tonight.

The *TIP* formula is easy to use. Let's apply it in introducing Sam Nobody.

"Ladies and gentlemen. Tonight we have a 40-minute presentation on how you can own your own business with no risk." (This is the topic.)

"I am sure each one of you would like the additional security and the increased standard of living an extra income allows." (This is why it is important to our listeners.)

"We are very fortunate to have with us tonight a man who has been successful in his own business. He has presented and helped many people start their own part-time businesses over the past 3 years. He is a true expert on how to get started, so please let me introduce Mr. Sam Nobody!" (This is the person.)

There is really nothing to it. The *TIP* formula is direct and gives the speaker a head start on credibility with the audience. And wouldn't you want the audience to like and believe the speaker at your opportunity meeting?

The easy *TIP* introduction will avoid the boring and sometimes disastrous introductions that can kill your audience.

Keeping your downline

Is the key to multilevel success being a great recruiter? Just sponsor plenty of distributors and watch the checks roll in? What if a leader spent 100% of his time recruiting and prospecting?

Total focus on recruiting new distributors will ruin the very group that leaders try to build. There is an old saying, "Many MLM leaders throw new distributors on the front of the wagon as fast as they fall out the back." While a leader recruits new distributors, his old, untrained distributors become discouraged and drop out of the program.

A key to a profitable multilevel business is not getting more distributors, but keeping the present distributors.

Here are three steps that help keep your downline active:

STEP 1: Money. Most new distributors join to improve their financial status. Exciting opportunity meetings cater to their desire and promise a new life of riches and financial security. What are the chances of a brand new distributor becoming a superstar and making thousands of extra dollars during the first couple months? Razor slim.

Like any new profession, training and foundation-building comes first. The riches come later. In 30 to 90 days, your new distributor will realize there is no free lunch. Large bonus checks come from large product volumes, not excitement and opportunity meeting promises.

The MLM leader will lose his new distributors in 30 to 90 days unless he phases his new distributors into Step 2.

STEP 2: Products. The majority of distributors in MLM do not make large bonus checks. A leader fails if he attempts to keep his distributors loyal through bonus checks alone. True leaders believe that product loyalty will keep their distributors active long after the mirage of instant wealth has evaporated. This raises the question: How do distributors get product loyalty? They don't get it from the company, but from their leaders. Leaders fail when they mistakenly believe that it is their company's sole responsibility to recruit, motivate, and train their distributors. If the company is willing to do all that, why would they need distributors? Most knowledgeable leaders use some, if not all, of the following methods to train and inspire their distributors concerning the company product line:

A. Product knowledge in cassette tapes

B. Product highlights in distributor newsletters

C. Testimonial sharing during opportunity meetings

D. Conducting product rallies and training

STEP 3: Leadership. The last and most powerful way to "lock in" distributors is to acknowledge the person's mental needs as a leader. Most average individuals go through life unwanted, unnoticed, and unappreciated. As leaders, we can fill these voids in our distributors' lives and earn their undying loyalty. Too many amateur leaders are only after what they want. They are not thinking of the needs and/or wants of their distributors. When leaders appear selfish, their distributors go elsewhere. The effective leader should:

(1) empathize with his distributors' personal problems

(2) give recognition

(3) help them reach their personal goals.

This way, he keeps his downlines active and loyal.

These three simple steps help leaders build and keep a solid, effective, and productive organization.

Do you want more great recruiting ideas?

Visit us on the web:

http://www.fortunenow.com

Or write to:

KAAS Publishing
P.O. Box 890084
Houston, TX 77289
(281) 280-9800

Want to sponsor more distributors? Want to sponsor better distributors? Want to build an incredible large and stable MLM organization?

Big Al's MLM Sponsoring Secrets album contains the very best recruiting techniques for you and your downline. The information is awesome and easy to use.

Get eight CDs with Big Al's best recruiting secrets. Plus, you get <u>four additional</u> CDs with his basic training workshop, *Big Al Live in London* — free. The entire set of 12 audio training CDs can be ordered by contacting:

Here are four more *Big Al Recruiting Books* you'll want in your library:

#1 *Big Al Tells All, The Recruiting System (Sponsoring Magic).* This is the original Big Al classic that details the entire Big Al Recruiting System. You'll learn about:

♦ Locating and qualifying new prospects
♦ Closing before you start your presentation
♦ The magic two questions
♦ Making fear of loss work for you
♦ The dairy farm syndrome
♦ The 25-minute presentation that works
♦ Strawberries as a selling tool
♦ Ridding your organization of the ten deadly myths
♦ And much, much more

If you were to read only one Big Al book, this should be your first choice.

#3 *Turbo MLM.* Accelerate your group-building with this third book in the *Big Al* Recruiting Series. Turbocharge your recruiting methods by using:

♦ The million dollar close
♦ Mail order recruiting
♦ Handling money handicaps
♦ Sorting for true leaders
♦ Tale of two winners
♦ Dangers of over training
♦ Why prospects don't join

And, the all-time super income builder: *The Presentation Ratings Game.*

#4 *How To Build MLM Leaders For Fun & Profit.*
Build massive downline organizations by building independent motivated leaders. Your group is only as strong as its leaders. Special sections on:

- ◆ Cloning superhuman leaders
- ◆ The $93,000 Recruiting System
- ◆ Piggy-back your opportunity
- ◆ Ninja mail
- ◆ The file drawer method
- ◆ Hype from the top
- ◆ The 2% myth
- ◆ How to get all the prospects you want
- ◆ Streamlining your business for extra profit
- ◆ Man Kills Family Pet principle
- ◆ And much, much more

Just pick from the many easy methods and systems to build your leader network fast.

#5 *Super Prospecting: Special Offers & Quick-Start Systems.*
Put your new distributor to work in less than three minutes with the A.S.K. recruiting system, starting on page 77. This no-wait system makes recruiting easy for shy, busy, or brand new distributors. Special sections on:

- ◆ How to turn ordinary people into eager prospects
- ◆ The introvert's way to getting opportunity presentations
- ◆ The secret word in great offers
- ◆ What if your entire recruiting promotional budget was only $600?
- ◆ Guidelines for your personal audiocassette tape
- ◆ Sample script for your audiocassette tape
- ◆ And much, much more

Make your offers irresistible, get prospects to come to you. It may be the best *Big Al* book ever published!

Volume Discounts

All *Big Al* Recruiting Books are $12.95 each.

For the professional leader who wishes to take advantage
of *Big Al's* surprisingly generous quantity discounts,
please contact:

KAAS Publishing
P.O. Box 890084
Houston, TX 77289 USA

http://www.fortunenow.com

Visa, MasterCard, Discover and American Express orders
Phone (281) 280-9800

How To Give A
One-Minute
Presentation

By Tom Schreiter

Learn how to get a presentation appointment with 100% of the prospects you talk to, and give your prospects a COMPLETE presentation in only one minute!

Stop doing network marketing the hard way.

Learn the two sentences that will get your prospects to literally beg you for an instant presentation.

Learn how to give a complete, total, beginning-to-end presentation in only one minute!

And watch your prospects' eyes light up when they see how easy it is.

To order this 3-CD audio album, contact:

KAAS Publishing
P.O. Box 890084
Houston, TX 77289 USA

http://www.fortunenow.com

Visa, MasterCard, Discover and American Express orders
Phone (281) 280-9800

Feel a bit shy when approaching strangers? Would you like to turn acquaintances into hot, eager prospects? How can you approach potential prospects about your business without looking like a greedy salesman searching for a quick commission?

How To Get Rich Without Winning The Lottery, by Keith Schreiter is easy to read, easy to implement, and shows how anyone, a carpenter, a rocket scientist, a housewife, or even a lawyer (gasp!) can follow the simple principles to accumulate wealth. And the best part is that this book will show your prospects how to add network marketing to their wealth plan if they wish.

This is a gift that will build a long-term relationship. So leave a copy of this book with that cab driver who gave you good service, to that hotel employee who helped you set up your opportunity meeting, to the waitress with the million-dollar smile, and to your best friend who would like to be rich, but doesn't knew how.

Once you read this book, your life will never be the same. You'll be on the direct road to financial independence even without the help of network marketing. And because you already do network marketing, you'll be way ahead on this million-dollar road to riches. The book is so good, you won't want to give away your personal copy.